Amplify Learning: A Global Collaborative

Amplifying Authentic Learning in Reading, Writing, and Mathematics

#AMPGLOBALEDU

MATTHEW RHOADS

BECKY LIM

EduMatch
PUBLISHING

We dedicate this book to educators around the world. You inspire us as lifelong learners and as educators to continue to improve and learn so we can amplify student learning!

AMPLIFY LEARNING: A GLOBAL COLLABORATIVE SERIES

Amplify Learning: A Global Collaborative is a book series about integrating instructional strategies with EdTech tools to amplify learning written and compiled by educators throughout the world. Compiled and edited by two EdTech experts, innovators, and coaches, Matthew Rhoads and Becky Lim recruited K-16 educators from across the world to write a chapter of their area of expertise in integrating instructional strategies with EdTech tools to amplify their instruction and student learning. To learn more about the book series, check out www.AmpGlobalEdu.com for information.

BOOK 1 - AMPLIFYING INSTRUCTIONAL DESIGN

Within the first book of the series, *Amplifying Instructional Design* covers an assortment of engagement, collaboration, assessment, and feedback strategies integrated with EdTech for any classroom setting. By reading through each of these strategies and EdTech integrations, you will have a toolkit and repository of strategies that you can use to create any type of lesson within any classroom setting. Amplify your student learning and instruction by taking these practical and applicable strategies and integrations into the classroom and school by tried and true integrations from educators across the world.

BOOK 2 - AMPLIFYING AUTHENTIC READING, WRITING, AND MATHEMATICS

The second book of the series, *Amplifying Authentic Reading, Writing, and Mathematics* covers several instructional strategies integrated with EdTech tools to amplify student learning in these key content areas. Teachers will be provided with a toolkit of practical and applicable instructional strategies that can be utilized across any grade level to build student skills within in-person, online, and blended learning classroom settings. Strategies in this book will be illustrated utilizing a wide range of EdTech tools that are available in classrooms from around the world. Readers will be able to come to this book, again and again, to build their instructional toolkit to meet the needs of their ever-changing classroom and student needs.

BOOK 3 - AMPLIFYING STUDENT INQUIRY IN ROBOTICS, COMPUTER SCIENCE, AND STEAM

The third book of the series, *Amplifying Student Inquiry in Robotics, Computer Science, and STEAM* provides teachers with a toolkit of strategies to teach Robotics, Computer Science, and STEAM using a variety of EdTech tools. The instructional strategies and EdTech tool integrations illustrated in this book meet the needs of growing student skills across content areas that help power our modern world.

Teachers will see examples of how they can conduct cross-curricular lessons as well as put students in the position to learn the foundations of coding to create, empower, and even control robots. Readers will be able to see examples of the strategies provided in action as well as be provided with additional resources to help them plan and execute the lessons.

BOOK 4 - AMPLIFYING DIVERSE LEARNING NEEDS

The fourth book of the series, *Amplifying Diverse Learning Need*, provides teachers with a toolkit of strategies to differentiate and personalize instruction while integrating EdTech toosl to amplify student learning for diverse and multilingual learners. Strategies and EdTech integrations discussed in this book are geared towards providing teachers and diverse learners opportunities to provide optimal instruction within online, blended, and in-person classroom settings to meet students individual learning needs. Teachers will be able to take a multitude of strategies discussed back to their classroom to help further differentiate lessons through multiple modalities and EdTech supports and personalize them to meet each student where they are at.

CONTENTS

AMPLIFY LEARNING: A GLOBAL COLLABORATIVE

AMPLIFYING AUTHENTIC LEARNING IN READING, WRITING, AND MATHEMATICS

As educators look to improve their practice, grow in their field, and bring new strategies into their classroom, the best resource to rely on is other educators. Teaching is not meant to be done in a silo. Fortunately, teachers near and far have tried-and-true strategies to share with both rookie and veteran teachers through authentic professional development and via the internet.

Thanks to technology and our interconnected world, educators can now collaborate and learn from others across different time zones.

Education continues to evolve at a rapid pace and, in the process, educators are tasked with staying up to date on the latest research-based best practices, EdTech integrations, and Social-Emotional Learning (SEL) strategies. To ensure that students are receiving a well-rounded, career and college ready education, educators go out of their way to keep up with the research and provide students with learning experiences that are meaningful and impactful. We live in a day and age where careers are constantly changing and the need for genuine connections, along with a strong background in utilizing technology, is now the standard in K-12 classroom settings. Genuine connections take place when authentic learning is prevalent in the daily learning environment.

Incorporating authentic learning into the classroom setting and tying it in with EdTech ensures that we are reaching students where they are. Authentic learning is all about the learner. Students deserve opportunities to explore, engage in genuine discussions, and make meaning out of concepts that involve real-world scenarios and situations that are both familiar and relevant to them. Gamification and projects are becoming more popular in the classroom because students have voice and ownership of their learning. While gamification and projects are not the only forms of authentic learning, they are both commonly found in reading, writing, and math classrooms around the world. Ultimately, students deserve to understand the purpose behind the learning that is taking place in the classroom, in addition to having their voice amplified throughout the learning process.

"Content Without Purpose is Only Trivia."

— *STEVE REVINGTON*

WELCOME TO THE AMPLIFY LEARNING: A GLOBAL COLLABORATIVE SERIES

The *Amplify Learning: A Global Collaborative Series* is a set of four books that make up an incredible instructional toolkit for teachers, coaches, and school and district leaders that can be utilized to amplify the learning occurring within their classrooms, schools, and districts.

Additionally, the vast majority of the strategies and EdTech integrations discussed in this book, as well as the book series, can be implemented within almost every classroom setting imaginable.

Overall, each book within the series focuses on integrating instructional strategies with EdTech in a multitude of different areas that span much of the skills and content that are taught to students in school.

- Book 1: Amplifying Instructional Design
- Book 2: Amplifying Authentic Learning in Reading, Writing, and Mathematics
- Book 3: Amplifying Student Inquiry in Robotics, Computer Science, and STEAM
- Book 4: Amplifying Diverse Learning Needs

PURPOSE OF THIS BOOK SERIES AND BOOK

Amplify Learning: A Global Collaborative series came from the ideas and connections generated from a Global Professional Learning Network (PLN). The hashtag **#bettertogether** comes to mind because as a collection of educators, we can work together across the world to amplify the learning of our students. As a result, both editor's, Matt Rhoads and Becky Lim, decided to come together and take this idea and crowdsource what we felt is a pivotal area in education: integrating instructional strategies with EdTech to amplify student learning. This manifested into *Amplify Learning: A Global Collaborative* book series, which is a collection of crowdsourced books on this topic from educators across the world who are teachers, instructional coaches, and instructional leaders. Together, we feel we can make a positive impact by bringing together our expertise to navigate and thrive in our ever-changing world of education through the work we are doing in this book series.

Specifically, Book Two of the *Amplify Learning: A Global Collaborative* series is on *Amplifying Authentic Learning in Reading, Writing, and Mathematics.* This book focuses on the three key instructional content areas of reading, writing, and mathematics that can be integrated with EdTech to amplify student learning. The instructional strategies and integrations provided in each of these content areas can be integrated with mainstream EdTech tools to provide top-of-the-line instruction within online, blended, and fully in-person classroom settings. Going further, the research-based strategies and EdTech integrations discussed in all three chapters of this book will arm you with a toolkit of strategies that can support you in creating engaging, innovative, and research-based instruction that can bring out your students strengths and creativity as they learn reading, writing, and mathematical skills. This is what authentic learning looks like, as we want our students to demonstrate their strengths, confidence, and creativity as a result of the instructional actions we take to amplify their learning. Thus, by having a firm hold on providing effective instruction in each of these content areas, we have the ability to build our students' foundational skills that are essential in navigating our ever-changing world.

THE EDITORS

As curators, EdTech innovators, editors, and practicing educators, we both bring our own perspectives and experiences in education to this book. As editors of this book, our backgrounds are important to note, as we will be providing commentary throughout each chapter. While this book's purpose is to highlight the diversity of teachers and instructional strategy integrations with EdTech, we will provide our own insight throughout each of the chapters as to why these strategies and integrations are essential to amplify learning.

Matthew Rhoads, Ed.D. Dr. Rhoads is an EdTech innovator, an expert in data literacy and data-driven decision-making, and integrating instructional strategies with EdTech tools. At the beginning of his education career, he focused on blended learning and EdTech integration to amplify student learning. He taught English, Math, and Social Sciences at the secondary level in Special Education and General Education settings. Each of these opportunities gave Dr. Rhoads time to experiment, refining strategies and routines integrated with EdTech tools to amplify instruction and learning. Currently, he serves as an EdTech integrationist and coach that oversees six schools in North San Diego County. Additionally, Dr. Rhoads has taught at the university level with a focus on EdTech integration as well as supervised and coached new teacher candidates. His latest book is *Navigating the Toggled Term: A Guide for K-12 Classroom and School Leaders*. More information on Dr. Rhoads and his work can be found at www.matthewrhoads.com.

Becky Lim, M.Ed. As a mentor and leader in education, Becky aims to create a positive and sustainable impact across education! She is an innovative and passionate Digital Learning Coach that serves to support teacher and student growth. Becky transitioned from an elementary school teacher to a coach, where she currently supports elementary teachers district-wide. With a Master's in educational leadership and a graduate certificate in Instructional Technology, Becky uses her skills to drive meaningful EdTech integration. She works with educators globally as a Global Google Educator Group leader and leads #ECOpenChat (a coach's open chat group and book study). More information on Becky Lim can be found at www.techwithbecky.com.

DIVERSITY OF CONTRIBUTING AUTHORS

To ensure that we are broadening our skills and mindset, we intentionally handpicked leaders in education from around the globe to amplify their voices for this book series. Each contributing author brings their own dynamic style and perspective to their respective chapter. To grow our practice in education, it is critical to learn from educators outside of our network. We will be provided with research and strategies from a variety of different grades, content areas, and cultures. While each strategy may not directly align with the work you are doing in your classroom, we hope that you will find cross-connecting concepts and new ideas to support your student's diverse learning needs.

This particular book showcases the work of three amazing educators from the United States and the United Kingdom. Each bringing in their own expertise and perspective, the strategies shared are unique and original, while continuing to bring in supporting research and an openness to cross-curricular uses.

MEET THIS BOOK'S CONTRIBUTING AUTHORS

For this book on *Amplifying Authentic Learning in Reading, Writing, and Mathematics,* the educators were selected from two different regions of the United States and one from the United Kingdom, but carry the experience of teaching abroad and within diverse urban and suburban settings. Each of these authors carries years of experience in education working in the classroom, as instructional coaches, and as Directors of Educational Technology.

Jennifer Toney, Ph.D., the author of the first chapter on reading, has extensive expertise in blended learning and literacy instruction. Additionally, her research interests include multimodal composition and reading in the elementary classroom and developing an elementary curriculum for grades K-5. As a practicing elementary teacher, she has taught in grades K-3 and enjoys focusing on building students' reading and writing abilities in critical learning phases of their academic careers.

Janet Ilko, Ed.D., the author of the second chapter on writing, has over three decades of teaching experience spanning all of K-12. Additionally, she has been an instructional coach, ELD teacher, classroom teacher, and program manager of an independent studies program. Her research focus was on strategies to support the language development of long-term English learners. She has a passion for teaching writing and is a member of the National and San

Diego Writing Projects. In her writing strategies, rigor, and relevancy are extremely important to encourage student engagement, buy-in, and creativity.

Sammy White, the author of the third and final chapter on mathematics, has spent years developing mathematics curricula and has helped teachers improve their mathematical instruction through the strategies she successfully utilized during her time in the classroom. Her goal is to embed mathematics across the school's curriculum, so it is incorporated throughout the school day rather than during a single time block. As the first female Google for Education Coach in Europe and Innovator, her expertise is to integrate technology with the strategies she's honed to amplify student learning.

"What separates good content from great content is a willingness to take risks and push the envelope."

— BRIAN HALLIGAN

OVERVIEW OF CHAPTERS - AMPLIFYING AUTHENTIC LEARNING IN READING, WRITING, AND MATHEMATICS

As you navigate this book, you may notice that the chapters are not organized in any specific order. This is for a good reason. We want you to navigate this book to meet your instructional curiosities and needs related to teaching reading, writing, and mathematics.

Remember, the strategies and integrations outlined in each chapter can be utilized across different content areas. As a result, when you are reading this book, not only think about how the strategies and integrations may be utilized for a specific content area, but for all content areas.

Ultimately, you can always use this overview of chapters as your landing page to help map out your reading journey. Provided here are the abstracts of the chapters included in this book from our contributing authors teaching around the world. Each abstract summarizes the chapter and the instructional theme, including the instructional strategies and EdTech integrations discussed.

Each chapter incorporates a similar layout to provide consistency while still giving authenticity to each contributing author's voice. Before diving into EdTech tools and implementation, chapters will begin with research to give insight into theoretical concepts behind a strategy and validations of tools. Following the research will be the strategies and real-world application of each research-based strategy and EdTech tool integration. Provided is a quick overview of each chapter incorporated in this book.

Chapter 1: Authentic Learning in Reading - By: Jennifer Toney, Ph.D.

Reading is an essential skill all teachers need to be teaching and reinforcing. Utilizing a wide range of strategies like reciprocal teaching, direct instruction, station rotation, spaced vs. mass practice, and digital anchor charts, this chapter is geared towards strategies and EdTech integrations that can help teachers teach reading to students of all grades. Integrating tools such as interactive video, bulletin boards, and text differentiators, there are a number of integrations that are provided to teach reading in any setting to amplify reading instruction and student learning.

Chapter 2: Authentic Learning in Writing - By: Janet Ilko, Ed.D

Within this chapter, Dr. Ilko provides a framework for teaching writing in digital spaces as well as through multiple mediums to empower student voice and agency. Writing feedback, student personalization, and sharing writing and content on social media and digital portfolios are discussed. This chapter has a number of examples that model how the writing instruction takes place and has a highly personal perspective showing how writing is a gradual process that can then manifest itself in many ways when it's published.

Chapter 3: Authentic Learning in Mathematics - By: Sammy White

In this chapter that is geared towards mathematics, you will learn not only a number of strategies to amplify your mathematics instruction but instruction teaching across all concepts and skills. Modeling, retrieval practice, and strategic practice are the main strategies and themes discussed in the chapter, along with integrating those strategies with a number of EdTech tools to create bite-sized learning experiences and practice opportunities.

HOW TO USE THIS BOOK

Ultimately, we want readers of this book to read this book and then come back to the chapters again and again for the content you would like to focus on to amplify your instruction. As discussed earlier, each of the strategies and integrations discussed in this book is interchangeable for teaching all areas of content. For this reason, we want you to focus on several different factors while you are reading the book to support your instructional integration needs in your classroom. Each factor discussed here is to help frame the context of how to use this book. Our goal is to support you in your journey to find the best instructional strategy integrations from educators across the globe. These five factors to think about while reading this book include: educational context, cognitive load, and EdTech integrations that can be adjusted to your setting, think less is more when selecting strategies and integrations, and watch out for notes from the editors along the way. Editor notes will provide analysis and commentary that may further support you in your journey.

EDUCATIONAL CONTEXT - MANY VARIABLES AT PLAY

Everyone's context in education is different and unique, as they may be teaching in a different country, region, education system, and classroom setting. You may be teaching fully in person, online, or within a blended learning setting. Additionally, your classroom instructional setting and school setting may change from year to year as you progress through your career. At the classroom level, the group of students, teachers, instructional strategies, classroom setting, location of the school, and the resources they have available, are all ever-changing variables. All classrooms have unique characteristics that can never be completely replicated. There are many variables that come into play, and it creates very unique classroom settings and environments, which makes education very special. With this said, nothing will ever appear exactly the same from classroom to classroom and school to school. Yet, we want to emphasize that most strategies and EdTech integrations can be adjusted and adapted to meet your instructional and student needs, as they may change from moment to moment, lesson to lesson, or over the course of the school year. Thus, as you read each chapter of the book and books within the book series, consider your context in education and how you can adjust and adapt the strategies outlined to meet your students' diverse learning needs.

COGNITIVE LOAD - SOMETHING WE CANNOT EVER OVERLOOK

Cognitive load relates to the capacity of our brain's working memory that is used while processing information that is being presented to learners. Cognitive load is essential to know about because we as humans and learners can only process so much information at once to then be transferred from our short-term memory to our long-term memory. As educators, this is something we must be aware of as we provide instruction and integrate technology to deliver our instruction, because learning new information and processing that information requires a mental effort. This mental effort, our cognitive load, affects how information is processed in our working memory.

Cognitive load affects our students' learning outcomes because our working memory has only so much capacity to take on new information. This results in our ability to complete tasks and multi-task. Think about when we give our students too many steps and they get confused.

Ultimately, when our cognitive load is high and we are bombarded by too many steps and multi-tasking scenarios, learning is much more difficult. If we have too much information to process in our working memory, long-term memories will have difficulty forming.

As educators, we want to decrease our student's cognitive load that may impede deep thinking and learning. We provide examples of what increases cognitive load and decreases cognitive load. Examples of scenarios that can increase our students' cognitive load include not providing enough background information and context before jumping into a lesson, increasing the task's complexity, or the number of steps involved in completing the task. To decrease the amount of cognitive load on our students is to activate prior knowledge, provide context, and utilize your students' strengths while teaching them something new, and decreasing the number of steps our tasks require (Leahy & Sweller, 2008). The last facet discussed on the number of steps required to complete a classroom instructional task is important to think about as we integrate EdTech along with our instructional strategies to amplify our students' learning. As discussed in *Amplifying Instructional Design* as well as this book and book series, the theme of "think less is more" is as important as ever when thinking about cognitive load and student learning.

Keep this in mind as you read this book and book series, as it will be key to successful instructional and learning outcomes!

LESS IS MORE WHEN SELECTING STRATEGIES AND INTEGRATIONS

As you learn more strategies and EdTech integrations to amplify student learning in reading, writing, and mathematics, the goal is to pragmatically evaluate which ones will work the best for you and your students. Ultimately, when it comes down to it, be judicious in selecting the strategies because we want you to focus on successfully implementing three to five strategies and integrations versus trying out ten to fifteen strategies at a surface level. Additionally, when we focus on implementing many strategies at once, they tend to be harder to practice and improve. Thus, having the "less is more" mindset and being aware that you can always come back again and again to the chapters. By doing this, you can further explore strategies and integrations that intrigued you after you have had time implementing and practicing the initial ones you have selected into your classroom.

Overall, this book is meant to be read more than once and be a continued reference for you. Get started by focusing on the strategies and integrations that will best amplify your instruction and students in your current classroom setting. Then, after some time of reflection and planning, think about how you can use the strategies and integrations in the future.

JOIN OUR GLOBAL COMMUNITY #AMPGLOBALEDU

To promote community, connectivity, and creativity on a global level, we want to take the learning beyond the pages of this book. Twitter provides opportunities for educators to connect, share, and grow from one another. Join our Professional Learning Network (#PLN) by following #AmpGlobalEdu on Twitter. Our #PLN focuses on amplifying educator voices and opening the door for global transformation in education. We also want to learn from you. As you are reading, trying on new ideas, and discovering new strategies and EdTech integrations, share them with our community on Twitter using #AmpGlobalEdu in your post. Together, we can amplify the learning of the greater educational community to impact student learning across the world.

WATCH OUT FOR NOTES FROM THE EDITORS IN EACH CHAPTER

Throughout the book, you will notice notes from the editors. Each note is in place to provide commentary and further analysis related to the chapter's content. As editors, we bring our individual expertise and experiences in education to the table. As a result, our goal is to further support and help you integrate

strategies and EdTech tools within your classroom setting. We will provide additional ideas, examples of how various strategies can be integrated, perspectives, and provide diagrams and tables relating to the content being discussed in each chapter. When you see a speaker or amplification symbol in the book that says, "from the editors," this is what we are referring to here. Editor notes will arrive throughout and at the end of each chapter. Ultimately, our goal is to amplify the content discussed in the chapter. We do not want to take away from anything our contributing authors wrote. Rather, we are providing additional content and editorials to amplify the learning that is taking place!

CHECK OUT ADDITIONAL EDTECH STRATEGIES FROM EDUCATORS AROUND THE WORLD

At the conclusion of each chapter, you will also notice strategies and tools from educators across the world. Each of these notes outlines a particular strategy and EdTech tool integration.

We wanted to provide opportunities to include more voices and their expertise to amplify the content discussed in this book, along with the voices of the educators. Educator notes will appear at the end of each chapter, which will provide even more opportunities for our learning to be amplified throughout the book.

LET'S GET STARTED!

Authentic learning in reading, writing, and mathematics is the foundation of teaching twenty-first-century skills for our students to be lifelong learners. In this same light, we must provide opportunities to not only learn foundational skills but to provide creative and innovative opportunities for students to share their voices while engaged in the learning. This agency students gain from these opportunities helps build self-confidence for them to be authentically who they are and express themselves through multiple modalities.

Educators now have the strategies and tools for students to amplify how they learn how to read, write, and solve math problems. Fun and engaging lessons and strategies, along with outlets of student choice and modalities of content creation, create a recipe for success in our classrooms. Now, more than ever before, we have the toolkit to make this happen!

As you progress through this book, you can decide to move between the three chapters in whichever order you desire. The strategies and integrations can be interchangeable. When presented with integrations, try to reflect, and think about how they can be utilized in your classroom, school, and district. Hopefully, after reading and reflecting, a feeling of empowerment and inspiration comes about. For us, it creates immense excitement. It made us want to come back to each chapter time and time again to analyze the strategies and integrations and implement them for our teachers and students!

The people who are crazy enough to think they can change the world are the ones who do.

— *STEVE JOBS*

Amplifying Authentic Learning

- **Chapter 1: Authentic Learning in Reading - By: Jennifer Toney, Ph.D.**

- **Chapter 2: Authentic Learning in Writing - By: Janet Ilko, Ed.D.**

- **Chapter 3: Authentic Learning in Mathematics - By: Sammy White**

Chapter 1: Authentic Learning in Reading

By: Jennifer Toney, Ph.D

United States of America

"Authentic reading experiences with EdTech integration offer such techniques that many learners now crave in order to achieve reading comprehension success."
- Jennifer Toney, Ph.D

WHY YOU SHOULD READ THIS CHAPTER

Y ou should read this chapter because each and every teacher is a reading teacher.

Regardless of age, the ability to read is a life-changing skill. Reading allows us to explore and understand our world. Foundationally, it allows us the ability to learn additional skills and build our knowledge bank as we progress through our education. All teachers teach reading in one form or another because reading is the foundational skill underpinning all we learn. Since we are all reading teachers who reside in modern-day classrooms without boundaries, it's important to build our repertoire of reading strategies and integrate them with EdTech tools to provide students with reading instruction within online, blended, and traditional in-person classroom settings. Therefore, it is imperative for us to always be on the lookout to improve how we teach reading.

Students of all ages and grade levels can improve their reading ability. This chapter dives into helping students, regardless of grade level, to build their reading comprehension skills.

Reading comprehension strategies, ranging from spaced vs. mass practice, digging deeper into the story's topics, and reciprocal teaching are among many strategies outlined. Going beyond the research-based strategy itself, various EdTech tools and lesson focuses and plans are shown to demonstrate how the strategy and EdTech tools are integrated to amplify student learning.

As you progress through the chapter, your reading instructional toolkit will be expanded along with how to further integrate those strategies with mainstream EdTech tools. Furthermore, regardless of what grade level and content you may teach, each of these strategies and integrations can be utilized. Last, you will see how Dr. Toney takes a step-by-step approach to how she aligns the reading strategy with the learning focus in addition to integrating the strategy within the context of a lesson. This will help you facilitate the reading strategy in your classroom as it provides an illustrative model of how to do this effectively.

AUTHENTIC LEARNING IN READING

Reading is a vital component to becoming a literate, contributing twenty-first-century citizen.

There are a variety of purposes of reading, one of which is to create. Whether our aim is to create meaning, a connection, an impact, an original work, an escape, an emotion, or an understanding; we read to create. Now, over two decades into the twenty-first century, creating has become an expectation of readers (NCTE, 2019). Yet, many readers struggle to create. Because often for readers to create, they must comprehend.

Although current educational standards suggest learning outcomes focused upon higher order thinking and in-depth understanding, merely stating these learning outcomes does not mean that all students will magically meet the written expectations. In fact, it is very difficult to create if there is little to no understanding of the text (Texas Education Agency, 2002). And that is the situation for many readers today. According to the National Center for Education Statistics (2020) only 66% of fourth-grade students in the United States performed at or above the National Assessment of Educational Progress (NAEP) basic achievement level in reading. A number of students in American third-grade classrooms are showing signs of following this trajectory as well. And, despite the best efforts of educators across the globe to teach from a distance with the tools they had, educational setbacks from the COVID-19 pandemic did not help the situation (Engzell et al., 2021).

3

In order to combat a number of reading struggles, my school has implemented a version of the Multi-Tiered System of Support (MTSS) model. This model is designed to support student outcomes and integrates academic and behavioral supports. McREL.org (2015) explains, "... rather than problem-solving academics in one room and behavior in another, teams work together to consider how academic challenges may influence observed behaviors, and vice-versa..." I work with a tier-two group of readers five days a week, for forty minutes a day. Early in the year, we focus on strengthening foundational reading skills, reading fluency, and reading vocabulary through direct instruction and authentic reading practice. We have conversations about why we read and work toward diving more deeply into reading comprehension. Reading comprehension is one of the main building blocks with which readers create. Therefore, although all parts of reading instruction are important, the focus of this chapter will be reading comprehension.

"Reading comprehension is one of the main building blocks with which readers create."

When I shifted from a self-contained elementary classroom to an intermediate level, departmentalized, English Language Arts (ELA) classroom, I knew I wanted to offer a reading workshop experience for my third-grade students. During that same year, our district shifted to a standards-based report card. Not to mention, my grade level was the first year our students were required to take the standardized state assessment. With all of these pieces, I spent a summer developing a new curriculum map and units of study schedule. I follow the gradual release of responsibility model in my reading workshop. Each day I present a mini lesson during which I model comprehension strategies and skills. Following our mini lesson and read aloud, students spend time practicing the modeled strategy during small groups in a learning center/station rotation portion of class. Finally, students work independently to strengthen their reading comprehension during independent reading and work time. During this time, I visit students and confer with them about their progress. This chapter offers examples of strategies that fit naturally into this classroom framework.

A note from Becky: Response to Intervention (RTI) and Positive Behavior Intervention and Supports (PBIS) are commonly used as forms of MTSS in schools. Regardless of your school's system, or lack of, the strategies shared in this chapter can be utilized in all reading classrooms. Without the support of a reading intervention teacher/specialist, students can receive individualized support during station rotations, Daily 5, and in an I do-You do-We do model.

After living through a global pandemic, students of all ages have experienced learning with and through technology. In fact, EdTech integration in classrooms of all content areas has become more vital than ever before. Moreover, during this turbulent time in our world's history, a potential for greater learning loss in reading comprehension may have occurred for new and even experienced readers. Thus, teaching students to truly comprehend texts requires an intensified approach. Authentic reading experiences with EdTech integration offer such techniques that many learners now crave in order to achieve reading comprehension success.

But where do educators begin? Considering the work of Douglas Fisher, Nancy Frey, and John Hattie (2016), John Hattie (2012, 2015), Weston Kieschnick (2017), and Jennifer Serravallo (2015), this chapter will offer the combination of proven teaching and learning strategies with EdTech integration to promote authentic reading experiences for learners. These examples will make students' learning visible, truly engage them in reading comprehension, and amplify their learning to take them to new and inspiring levels.

"Authentic reading experiences with EdTech integration offer such techniques that many learners now crave in order to achieve reading comprehension success."

THE RESEARCH AND STRATEGIES

To begin, it is beneficial to apply the Bold School Framework for Strategic Blended Learning™ (Kieschnick, 2017) and identify the desired academic outcome(s). The overarching reading comprehension focus of this chapter is key ideas and details. Without determining the main idea of the text, readers may flounder in understanding how the pieces of a text fit together. By having a solid foundation in identifying what is important to remember, there is greater potential for readers to make sense of the text. Across all grade levels, kindergarten through grade twelve, the first standard listed in both reading literature and reading informational texts is key ideas and details (National Governors Association Center for Best Practices, Council of Chief State School Officers, 2010). At each learning level, readers are challenged to cite textual evidence to answer questions and explain text connections. Textual evidence of literature and informational texts for key ideas and details across grade and content areas will provide the learning goals that will drive the conversation and selection of specific strategies for the following sections in this chapter.

To guide students toward amplified learning, it is helpful to draw upon the research of Fisher, Frey, and Hattie (2016), Hattie (2015), and Serravollo (2015). For over a decade, John Hattie explored what works in schools to improve student learning by examining the results of more than fifteen years of research in education (2012). Each of his findings offers an effect size for student achievement. Fisher et al. (2016) offer a list of Hattie's (2012) 150 influences on student achievement along with their rank and effect size, then explore how the strategies apply to literacy instruction. It is important to offer a variety of learning opportunities for students that toggle among the different levels of learning: surface, deep, and transfer. Hattie (2012) notes, "...there needs to be a major shift from an over-reliance on surface information and a reduced emphasis that the goal of education is [only] deep understanding or development of thinking skills towards a balance of surface and deep learning..." (p. 77). Next, select strategies that fit naturally into the structure of the specific classroom, and choose to embed amplified versions of engaging strategies. In this case, two of Serravallo's (2015) strategies. Then consider aspects from Hattie's work that have a variety of effect size ratings to promote authentic reading. Considering a balance of surface learning, deep learning, and transfer learning (Fisher et al, 2016), this chapter will examine the following strategies:

1. Direct instruction (effect size: 0.59) of study skills (effect size 0.63), specifically text annotation, and Serravallo's (2015) strategy, "Dig Deeper to Find a Story's Topics" (p. 205).
2. The Station Rotation Model (Kieschnick, 2017) to incorporate spaced vs. mass practice (effect size: 0.71) of Serravallo's (2015) strategy, "What and So

What?" (p. 237), and interactive video (effect size: 0.52).

3. Reciprocal Teaching (effect size: 0.74.)

Direct Instruction

Kieschnick (2017) defines direct instruction as, more than lecturing—it's a choreographed, pre-planned series of events that come together to teach new information and support students through to mastery.... it must be done with intention, in alignment with academic goals, and include a few key components that help make sure you're connecting with students. (p. 94). When introducing students to new information and skills, direct instruction is a "go-to" strategy for many educators. Fisher et al. (2016) suggests the benefits of direct instruction when stating, "there are some things that have to be directly explained to students, especially when other methods are less effective or more time consuming" (p. 47). Direct instruction means sharing success criteria up front and communicating the learning intention(s) through modeling the learning outcomes and guiding students toward reaching success with practice and time to check for understanding and discuss the process.

"Direct instruction means sharing success criteria up front and communicating the learning intention(s) through modeling the learning outcomes and guiding students toward reaching success with practice and time to check for understanding and discuss the process."

Study Skills

With an effect size of 0.63, study skills—like annotating a text in context—help improve reading comprehension. Fisher et al. (2016) note, "guided annotation of text, including underlining, circling, and making margin notes, can improve student understanding of new knowledge..." (p. 58). One practice that can be utilized to model text annotation is close reading. Lehman and Roberts (2014) explain the CCSS's emphasis on close reading as "the reading, rereading, and analysis of text for the purpose of interpreting it (p. ix). Dating back to the 1920s, close reading is nothing new (Pearson & Cervetti, 2015). However, the focus on text interpretation emphasized by the CCSS has returned the spotlight to this type of reading. What was once the way college students and academics explored text, has now become the expectation of readers from the time they begin reading at the elementary level. Throughout the formative reading years, students work toward developing a set of skills that lead them to independently construct meaning from the text, and explain text-based evidence that supports their ideas.

A note from Matt: Now, we have many interactive tools to help students practice their reading skills. By using adaptive EdTech tools that focus on building reading comprehension, such as iReady, MobyMax, NewsELA, and Readtheory, we can not only have our students learn at their own personalized pathway, but also collect important data to help drive our future instruction to our students.

Serravallo's "Dig Deeper to Find a Story's Topics"

Close reading is based on text evidence rather than the reader's background knowledge and personal experience. Other researchers recognize the importance of interactions readers have with the text and individual interpretations of their reading experience (Rosenblatt, 1978; Serravallo, 2015). Although Serravallo (2015) agrees that interpretations must be rooted in the details of the text, she values interaction with the text because "it becomes about letting stories help us see our world, feel something, question our own beliefs" (p. 191). One way she suggests we help readers think about the text is through a strategy titled, "Dig Deeper to Find a Story's Topics"

(Serravallo, 2015, p. 205). To use this strategy, the teacher can introduce how to find and record information from a text during a whole group lesson. It helps readers find a story's theme by listing topics (usually one word) and then explaining why this might be a big topic in the text. Then, using the words students note, the teacher can guide the discussion toward the theme (a more complete idea about the book) of the text. In her book, she offers an example of an anchor chart on which words were recorded on sticky notes and examples from the text are written beside the topic word.

Station Rotation

Station rotation is a way for teachers to differentiate instruction and offer a variety of learning opportunities during a class period in any content area. Often referred to as learning centers at the elementary level, groups of students work at one station for a set amount of time, then travel to the next center when the time is up. Kieschnick (2017) suggests an ideal rotation design of three stations: 1. Interactive video, 2. Teacher-led instruction, and 3. Collaborative activities and stations (pp. 68-69). In an ELA classroom, another possibility for the inclusion of a fourth station is an independent reading center. To offer interaction "with an academic concept through a range of mediums and through both rigorous and relevant examples" (p.68) it is vital to consider the content of each station. In my classroom, the following strategies have been strategically selected to offer rigor and relevance to students following a three-station rotation model. All effect sizes come from Hattie's (2015) Visible Learning research.

1. Small-Group Learning (effect size 0.49)-- often beneficial as a teacher-led group to work on new content and/or a reading comprehension program (effect size 0.55).
2. Interactive Video (effect size 0.54)-- a small number of students engage with a two-to-four-minute video with questions embedded by the teacher.
3. Spaced vs. Mass Practice (effect size 0.6)--to be utilized at any of the three stations, but would likely construct the content of an interactive video or collaborative learning station because it is a review of previously learned information. One tool that can be used for spaced vs. mass practice is Serravallo's (2015) "What? and So What?" strategy.

There are a variety of ways to amplify learning in a teacher-led group that may or may not incorporate educational technology tools. In many cases, teacher-led groups are offline/analog. Therefore, since this book explores amplifying learning with technology tools, the focus of the station rotation options will be on the latter two strategies listed above.

Interactive Video

Essentially creating a clone of the teacher, this strategy offers a variety of options. Teachers are provided with an opportunity to go beyond showing a video unknowing if students were paying attention and/or learning. In this strategy, questions about the content of the video are embedded at checkpoints before students can continue viewing. Kieschnick (2017) explains two methodologies for strategic interactive video use: 1. Show & Tell and 2. Tell & Show. For reading comprehension instruction, the interactive video could be a teacher reading a text, then stopping throughout for students to answer questions—show and tell. Additionally, the teacher could also demonstrate a comprehension strategy in the video, have students follow along in a tangible book, then complete tasks in the book and alongside the video simultaneously. At the conclusion of the video, the teacher can share answers/examples to the work students completed—tell and show.

 *A note from Becky: Many free web-based services are available for both teachers and students to create quick, interactive videos. Both Flip and Screencastify Submit allow teachers to create and assign videos to students and students can respond to the video using audio, video, and/or visuals.*

Spaced vs. Mass Practice of Serravallo's "What? and So What?"

Spaced practice is when the practice/use of a concept is spaced over time, and mass practice is where learning of a concept is concentrated in a shorter amount of time (Kieschnick, 2017, p. 181). Both of these are useful in the classroom, and it is important to have a balance of both. In their article, *Spaced Retrieval: Absolute Spacing Enhances Learning Regardless of Relative Spacing*, Karpicke and Bauerschmidt (2011) explain that the human brain remembers information longer when the use of that information is spaced out over time. Therefore, it is useful for educators to offer spaced practice of concepts over the course of the school year. A way to do this is to revisit concepts and skills that were taught earlier in the year, during learning center time. For example, consider the weeks and months after a reading workshop unit focused on informational text reading comprehension and modeling how to determine main ideas and key details. Students can participate in collaborative practice of reading comprehension through Serravallo's (2015) "What? and So What?" strategy. This strategy offers an opportunity for learners to explore the main idea of nonfiction text and synthesize important information. They go beyond merely listing a topic, by explaining what the author is trying to say about the topic with text evidence. This can be done in a small group (and this is supported by an effect size of 0.59 for cooperative vs. individualistic learning), but this strategy could also be utilized at an independent reading center/assessment.

Reciprocal Teaching

Reciprocal teaching allows small groups of students to focus on reading comprehension through reading closely and using four specific tools: summarizing, questioning, clarifying, and predicting. Frey et al. (2016) note, "The teacher segments the text into smaller chunks, and students are taught to pause after reading each segment to discuss its content using these four strategies" (p. 98). Hattie (2015) discovered reciprocal teaching has a 0.74 effect size. Moreover, Palincsar (2013) discusses this strategy's effectiveness with a variety of student groups, such as English learners and students with disabilities. This strategy is best introduced to readers in separate lessons with teacher modeling, then followed by subsequent modeling and sessions for students to practice each step (Rosenshine & Meister, 1993). Then, after students have mastered each part, they can work more independently.

Table 1.1

Reading Comprehension Strategies

Reading Comprehension Strategies	
Research Proving Reading Comprehension Amplifies Student Learning	**Strategies**
Fisher, D., Frey, N., & Hattie, J. (2016). *Visible learning for literacy.* Thousand Oaks, CA: Corwin. Hattie, J. (2012). *Visible learning for teachers.* New York, NY: Routledge Hattie, J. (2015). The applicability of visible learning to higher education. *Scholarship of Teacher and Learning in Psychology,* 1(1) 79-91. Kieschnick, W. (2017). *Bold School.* Rexford, NY: International Center for Leadership in Education.	Direct Instruction - Study Skills
Rosenblatt, L. (1978). *The reader, the text, the poem: The transactional theory of the literary work.* Carbondale, IL: Southern Illinois University Press. Serravallo, J. (2015). *The reading strategies book.* Portsmouth, NH: Heinemann.	Direct Instruction- "Dig Deeper to Find a Story's Topics"

Hattie, J. (2012). *Visible learning for teachers*. New York, NY: Routledge Hattie, J. (2015). The applicability of visible learning to higher education. *Scholarship of Teacher and Learning in Psychology*, 1(1) 79-91. Kieschnick, W. (2017). *Bold School*. Rexford, NY: International Center for Leadership in Education.	Station Rotation- Spaced vs. Mass Practice
Serravallo, J. (2015). *The reading strategies book*. Portsmouth, NH: Heinemann.	Station Rotation- "What? And So What?"
Hattie, J. (2012). *Visible learning for teachers*. New York, NY: Routledge Hattie, J. (2015). The applicability of visible learning to higher education. *Scholarship of Teacher and Learning in Psychology*. 1(1) 79-91. Kieschnick, W. (2017). *Bold School*. Rexford, NY: International Center for Leadership in Education.	Station Rotation - Interactive Video
Fisher, D., Frey, N., & Hattie, J. (2016). *Visible learning for literacy*. Thousand Oaks, CA: Corwin. Hattie, J. (2012). *Visible learning for teachers*. New York, NY: Routledge Hattie, J. (2015). The applicability of visible learning to higher education. *Scholarship of Teacher and Learning in Psychology*, 1(1) 79-91. Kieschnick. W. (2017). *Bold School*. Rexford. NY: International Center for Leadership in Education. Palincsar, A. S. (2013). Reciprocal teaching. In J. Hattie & E. Anderman (Eds.), *International guide to student achievement* (pp. 369-371). New York, NY: Routledge.	Reciprocal Teaching

Each of the tried-and-true reading comprehension strategies that I have introduced offer ways for students to strengthen their reading comprehension and create, and each of them can be a part of a variety of ELA classroom designs. It is beneficial to begin with modeling. Direct instruction of study skills and specific strategies, such as Serravallo's (2015) "Dig Deeper to Find a Story's Topic" are two examples of demonstrating how to read closely to construct meaning for students. Following direct instruction, students can participate in station rotation.

This can be done every day, or one or two days per week. In the station rotation model, students work in small groups at different learning centers for a set amount of time. This is a time for students to review previously learned material, work with their teacher on new material, and utilize tools such as interactive video. Learning center time is an opportunity to consider Hattie's (2015) idea of spaced vs. mass practice. Additionally, since students are working in small groups, they can collaborate as they practice reading comprehension skills through strategies like "What? and So What?" (Serravallo, 2015).

The final piece of the many parts to the reading classroom is student mastery of the reading comprehension strategies. Students can demonstrate their mastery level of applying strategies to text through reciprocal teaching. By working with peers to predict what might happen in a text, then clarify, question, and summarize what they read in the text, it is clear to see why this strategy is highly effective for visible learning. Each of these strategies is powerful on its own, and have proven to be successful. However, when paired with purposeful educational technology tools, learning has the potential to be amplified tenfold! With an overview of these dynamic reading comprehension strategies in mind, it is time to consider how they can be combined with EdTech tools in the classroom.

"Students can demonstrate their mastery level of applying strategies to text through reciprocal teaching."

Strategy Integration with EdTech Tools and Instructional Application Vignettes

EdTech tools have changed the field of education and reading instruction. Since the technology boom of the 1990s more reading comprehension enhancing tools have become more widespread and available to teachers and students in many classrooms. First and foremost the goal of utilizing any tool or strategy should be learning success for all. EdTech offers access to thousands of texts of a variety of reading levels. This gives readers of all ages and stages the opportunity to explore many interests and options. Aside from the plethora of text resources that are available, EdTech tools provide a natural chance for collaboration. For many readers, interactions with others scaffold them to understand texts in new and different ways. The strategies mentioned in this chapter are some specific examples of how EdTech benefits reading comprehension instruction. Most of the tools and applications that will be discussed can be conducted within online, blended, and traditional class settings. They offer flexibility for teaching and learning across grade levels too.

Direct Instruction of Text Annotation and "Dig Deeper to Find a Story's Topic"

When students are learning how to annotate a text, it is necessary to provide explicit examples of how it is done. To teach my learners how to annotate a text, we gather together around a SMARTboard, interactive display. I share the text with them and demonstrate what it means to "talk to the text". When I was learning how to teach, transparencies were a big thing. I thought it was so cool how my professors could print an entire page of text on a clear piece of paper and then mark it up with a dry erase marker. I couldn't wait to get my own classroom!

Then, my bubble burst when I realized how much time it would take for me to make all of the transparencies I wanted to use in addition to all of my other responsibilities. (I did not have a budget for classroom supplies, so I had to make or buy everything myself.) A couple of years later, I was hired at a new school and my classroom was equipped with a SMARTboard. Oh, the possibilities! I still have my SMARTboard all of these years later, and it is a very helpful tool for direct instruction.

A note from Matt: With the help of digital whiteboards, teachers can now use their tablets to display the whiteboard on their students' screens or on the front projector. Several digital whiteboards include Canva, Zoom Whiteboard, Whiteboard.fi, WhiteboardFox, WhiteboardChat, Jamboard, and Slides.

Two EdTech tools that are helpful in classrooms for direct instruction of study skills are: Gale in Context and Readworks. To use Readworks, students can gather in a class meeting space, and the teacher can show them how to access the website and login. It is useful to create a demonstration student account so the teacher screen looks how the accounts will look when they begin to practice. To model study skills, the teacher reads the passage aloud and embeds a

think-aloud throughout the reading. It is beneficial to plan the think-aloud ahead of time, as it is strategic. Preplanning provides ideas for the teacher's demonstration annotations. Some common phrases I use as I model my thinking are:

- *I am wondering...*
- *This is important because...*
- *I am confused by this because...*
- *I agree/disagree with this because...*

I also demonstrate using the comprehension questions as tools to guide my notes by splitting my screen to show the reading comprehension question set beside the passage while I highlight and annotate.

I explain to my students that reading a text and annotating it is like having a conversation with the writer. Then, I demonstrate how to highlight and add comments. I explain that annotating helps me remember what I am reading, and my notes are useful when other people ask me questions about what I have read. As I read, I teach them how to click on specific words and highlight them in color. I also show them how to add a comment. One idea I suggest is to use different colors for annotation types. For example, if the annotation is a question the words are highlighted in green. A color-coded key on a poster or a bookmark is a helpful tool for readers too.

Figure 1.1

Text Annotation Student Bookmarks

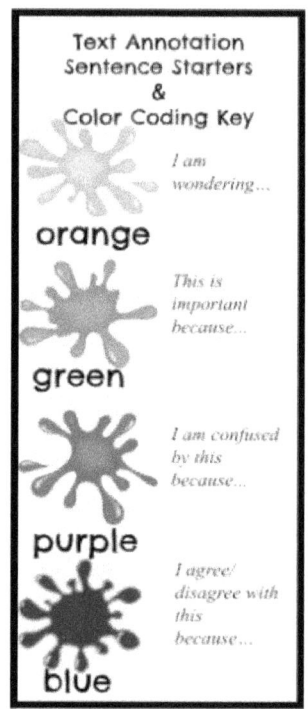

The Texas Education Agency (2021) and Elain K. McEwan (2021) suggest key comprehension strategies for highly effective reading. Of them, asking and answering questions, making connections, and inferring are listed. All of these, as well as the others that are listed in their writing can be accomplished through text annotation. Direct instruction of text annotation through Readworks helps amplify learning in a myriad of ways. I don't know about you, but there are many times when my students do not bring a pencil to class, let alone a variety of highlighters and sticky notes. Digital reading tools, such as Readworks, keep everything in one place! Not to mention it integrates seamlessly with Google Classroom, so I can post individualized assignments for my learners and see their progress as they work. After modeling and demonstrating how to read an article closely and annotate it, I can then demonstrate how to use the passage and notes to answer questions in a discussion group or on a written assignment. This also works in a traditional classroom setting, and it was extremely beneficial when I was teaching my readers online.

A note from Becky: NewsELA is another free digital resource that students can use to annotate real-world articles. Educators can create an account, find articles, adjust the articles to students' different reading levels, and assign tasks within the program. Bringing in up-to-date news articles supports and promotes global citizenship.

Table 1.2

Summary Lesson Example Showcasing Amplified Text Annotation

Learning Focus/Goal:	"Readers, today we are going to learn how to annotate text. Annotate means to write notes about what we are reading in the margins of the paper. Annotating is like having a conversation with the author of the text. We can do this in physical text and digital text. Today we will annotate a digital text."
Model:	Read and think aloud. Demonstrate thinking about and annotating on a www.readworks.org passage
Review/Send Off:	"Today we learned how to write notes about what we are reading in the margins of the paper to help us understand what we are reading. This is called annotating. Now you are going to... (go to your center for today or try this strategy on your own by logging in to the assigned text on www.readworks.org just like I showed you.)"

Along with text evidence and student interpretation, multimodal composition is beneficial for students to consider topics that point them to the theme of texts in the reading classroom (Cervetti, 2019; Wilkinson & Son, 2011). Another direct instruction lesson I share is how to design multimodal texts. There are two EdTech tools I use for this, Book Creator and Google Slides. I will share how I amplify Serravallo's (2015) strategy, *"Dig Deeper to Find A Story's Topics"*, through a collaborative Google Slide project. To model how to design and create multimodal slides I share a whole class chapter book read aloud. We discuss topic ideas and generate a list—I add each topic word to a new slide. As we are generating the list, we discuss evidence that supports each word. I explain that we can communicate through a variety of ways other than words. I choose one topic and explain my evidence from the book that matches it.

Next, I add something to the topic board. It can be an image, color, word, or even sound. Then I invite students to select a topic, share the text evidence, and suggest something to add to the board. We do this for as long as we need to until students have a grasp of the basic Google Slide tools. We also begin to discuss how the topic leads to the theme of the book. I add a sentence to the bottom of my example topic board that states the theme. After we read and record topics, in subsequent days, I share the Google Slides topic boards and meet with small groups.

They access the boards and add to the topic of their choosing with my guidance. Later, they can create their own topic boards during literature circles and book club time. Then, they discuss what the topic says about the theme and generate a sentence about the theme.

Figure 1.2

QR code of Multimodal Google Slide Topic Board Example for Al-Ling Louie's "Yeh Shen"

qrco.de/ampglobaledu20

Anchor charts are a reminder for students and a reference tool that some may use. However, many times the charts are forgotten as my students work to read and understand a text. By amplifying Seravallo's (2015) strategy, more students are able to be actively engaged in contributing their ideas about the text. For example, as students created the topic board that is pictured in this chapter they considered symbols that connected with specific examples from the book they were studying. After they selected the images, they thought about a font that matched their idea. Next, they reflected on what they added to the slide and wrote a sentence followed by their initials so others could ask questions and have a discussion. There are no sticky notes falling off of the wall or out of a book, and the topic boards are accessible from anywhere to all students in the classroom. Moreover, offering the multimodal component invites students to express their thoughts in creative ways while still considering text evidence.

Table 1.3

Summary Lesson Example Showcasing Amplified Serravallo's (2015) "Dig Deeper To Find A Story's Topic"

Learning Focus/Goal:	"Readers, today we are going to consider the big topics of our book and create class multimodal topic boards. We can communicate through a variety of ways other than words. Communicating with many modes helps us express our ideas in different ways."
Model:	Read and think aloud. Demonstrate thinking about a big topic and what text evidence made you think this is a topic of the text. Type the text on a blank slide and add a background color, words, images, sounds, GIFs, etc. that communicate the topic.
Review/Send Off:	"Today we learned how to think about the topic of a text and create a board that shows the topic. Now you are going to...(go to your center for today or try this strategy on your own by logging in to our shared slides and add your multimodal ideas to the assigned topic like I showed you.)"

Station Rotation for Spaced vs. Mass Practice and Interactive Video

Learning center time offers an excellent time for spaced practice of formerly learned material. Following direct instruction, students have time to work collaboratively, with the teacher, or independently on differentiated instructional tasks. An EdTech amplified reading comprehension strategy that can be spaced out for practice throughout the year is a teched out version of Serravallo's (2015) "What? and So what?" Google Site of nonfiction texts curated by students for students. Following our reading workshop unit on nonfiction texts, usually during the first semester of the year, students meet with a small group, and they read a nonfiction text. In their jot book, a notebook they keep with them as they read, they jot the possible "so what?" of the text. Then, they collaborate as a team to craft a linked page on a class Google Site. Student groups add one text title and its main idea to the site every month. The site is then shared with the next class of students the following year to provide examples of main ideas during the whole direction instruction lessons.

"What? and So What?" is a reading comprehension strategy that encourages students to look beyond a text's topic and synthesize the information to determine the main idea (Sarravallo, 2015). When students are invited to share their findings on a Google Site, their learning is amplified because their reading and thinking are being shared with others. There is a purpose beyond completing an assignment, students to become teachers of their peers. Moreover, Google Sites is a way for students to express their creativity as they share the main idea findings of the texts.

Table 1.4

Summary Lesson Example Showcasing Amplified Serravallo's (2015) "What? And So What?" For Spaced vs. Mass Practice

Learning Focus/Goal:	"Readers, today we are going to review the "What? And So What?" reading strategy that we learned a couple of months ago. You will read a nonfiction text with your reading club, then work together to add a new link to our Google Site. Continuing to practice this strategy will help you remember how to think deeply about a nonfiction text and communicate your ideas with others."
Model:	Read and think aloud. Demonstrate thinking about a big topic, what text evidence made you think this is a topic of the text, and explain the "so what?" piece that connects the topic to the theme. Review how to add a link to the Google Site and design the new link.
Review/Send Off:	"Today we reviewed how to think about the topic and theme of a text and share our thoughts on our class website. Now you are going to... (go to your center for today or work on this strategy on your own by logging in to our site and add creating a new link like I showed you.)"

I agree with Kieschnick's (2017) suggestion to embed an interactive video station during the rotation. This EdTech amplification allows me to clone myself through recording mini lessons. I use Screencastify to record my two-to-four-minute strategy demonstration. Students have the option to read a physical trade book or a digital text that aligns with the genre and/or strategy. After I record my video, I upload it to Edpuzzle so I can embed "stop and apply" checkpoints. When the video is ready, I upload a link on Google Classroom, so it is there for students to access during learning centers.

A Note from Matt: Interactive video can be incorporated into several forms of blended learning. Not only can it be a station within Station Rotation, but interactive video can also be an optimal instructional choice to utilize for the Flipped Classroom model. Specifically, to teach reading, an interactive video of the story or a preview of the story or text that will be read in class will provide students with the frontloaded context to help them comprehend the main ideas and key details of the text.

Interactive videos amplify learning because students are actively participating rather than simply watching a video. Edpuzzle offers a variety of settings, so students are required to complete specific tasks before they continue working. This feature is beneficial for student accountability during learning centers when I am working with a group of students at my teacher table. Interactive videos can be used to introduce new content and/or review previously learned content. The videos also allow the teacher to create an archive of lessons for students to revisit for as long as the video links are available.

Table 1.5

Summary Lesson Example Showcasing Amplified Interactive Video

Learning Focus/Goal:	"Readers, today we are going to learn how to use an interactive video for learning. Interactive videos are short videos that teach you how to do something, and they have stopping points so you can practice what you are learning."
Model:	Model watching, reading, thinking, and doing aloud by following the video. Demonstrate watching the clip then pausing to follow the embedded prompts.
Review/Send Off:	"Today we learned how to learn from an interactive video. Now you are going to... (go to your center for today or try this strategy on your own by logging in to the video link that I posted and work through the video lesson.)"

Reciprocal Teaching

During the reading workshop, students meet with their book clubs. At the start, each student is assigned a job such as predictor, summarizer, questioner, or clarifier so that they all contribute during the discussion. To amplify close reading and book clubs I have added a student podcast element. I provide a script for each episode that invites every student to add to the discussion of the book chapter. Students prepare the details of their section based on the focus of the episode. One student opens the episode by naming the title and author of the text, then summarizing the chapter the club members previously read. The next student offers questions the group had during discussion. Another clarifies and answers questions based on the text. And, a final show host offers the group's prediction

33

for the next chapter. The hosts base their show contribution on the text and the discussion their book club had prior to the podcast. I scaffold the podcast through a script, but older students can record the book club discussion without a script after they become comfortable with the reciprocal teaching elements.

There are a number of EdTech tools available to record podcasts, but my young students use Screencastify, Google Meets, and/or the Chrome Extension Simple Audio Recorder. I model how to record episodes with the whole class and with small groups to get everyone started. I also join in the conversation/recordings with each group until the students are able to conduct the groups completely independently. The student episodes can be made available on a class website for other students who would like to read the book and listen to the commentary.

When book clubs and literature circles are done well, students strengthen their reading comprehension through application (Daniels, 2002; Harvey & Daniels, 2015). Adding the podcast element amplifies learning because students are taking a leadership role and sharing their thoughts with others. Students become part of the production process, and learn to consider their audience as they discuss and develop the content of their shows. Furthermore, incorporating podcasting with reciprocal teaching offers an enjoyable authentic experience for readers and offers a real-world connection that makes their work more meaningful (Morgan, 2015).

Table 1.6

Summary Lesson Example Showcasing Amplified Reciprocal Teaching

Learning Focus/Goal:	"Readers, today we are going to learn how to produce podcast episodes. We have been working with our book clubs throughout the year and now we are going to follow a script to share our discussions with other students who are reading the same books as your clubs."
Model:	In a previous lesson, model how to fill in the script sections with notes from the book club conversation. In this lesson, model pressing the record button in the app and reading a prewritten script aloud that reviews a text that was previously shared with the class.
Review/Send Off:	"Today we learned how to record our book club podcast episode. Now you are going to... (go to your center for today or try this strategy on your own by meeting with your book club and recording your podcast episode.)"

Integrating research-based reading comprehension strategies with EdTech tools is important in today's ELA classrooms for students of all ages. First, consider the desired learning outcomes. Then, determine the most beneficial EdTech tool for students to use to reach this goal. In doing so, there is a potential for high effect learning to occur. There are strategies and tools to use in all stages of classroom instruction. Whether through direct instruction, small groups during station rotation, or individual and/or group independent work,

EdTech has the ability to amplify reading comprehension to a new level.

To amplify direct instruction of study skills like text annotation, www.readworks.org and www.newsela.com offer leveled passages that readers can highlight and annotate as they are searching for specific information. Educators can share passages with students in an in-person, blended, or virtual classroom. The passages can be read in a whole group setting and can spark dialogue among the teacher and students. In addition, Serravallo's (2015) reading comprehension strategy "Dig Deeper to Find A Story's Topic" is another strategy that can be modeled in a whole group, direct instruction setting. Multimodal composition can be integrated through the use of Google Slides. The teacher reads a text with the class, and they discuss the topics of the text.

Then, there is a demonstration of how to craft a multimodal interpretation of the text topic in a shared presentation.

Another format for learning in the classroom is interactive small groups in a station rotation model or learning centers. Along with a teacher-led center (often of new material), two other strategies to utilize during this time are spaced vs. mass practice and interactive video.

Students can work in a collaborative group to read a text and apply Serravallo's (2015) "What? and So What?" strategy to synthesize what they have read and record the main idea. Google Sites offers an opportunity for students to curate visually appealing resources for younger students to access as they learn how to determine the main idea of a nonfiction text. This can be an ongoing project to promote spaced practice of the reading comprehension skill determining the main idea of a text, recounting the key details, and explaining how they support the main idea.

Interactive video is another piece of the station rotation portion in a classroom learning community. Educators can create their own short videos, or share someone else's, and embed questions. This amplification offers endless opportunities for review and enrichment of reading comprehension strategies. This strategy is also another way to offer spaced practice of material throughout the school year, so students maintain the skills and strategies for the long term.

Finally, interactive videos can be assigned to students in any learning setting, and can be accessed on the internet. After teachers have explicitly modeled the strategies and offered time for students to practice the strategies, students can work independently. One way they can do this is to participate in reciprocal teaching in book clubs and produce a podcast for their peers. In this amplified strategy, book clubs meet to read texts then summarize, question, clarify and predict the chapter. They use the information from their discussion to complete a script, then record a podcast episode to share on a classroom website.

CONCLUSION - AUTHENTIC LEARNING IN READING

In 2019, under 45% of fourth graders in the United States demonstrated proficiency in reading (National Center for Education Statistics, 2020). Without an improvement in understanding texts, readers will continue to miss out on understanding important information. They will struggle in trying to incorporate critical and higher order thinking skills into their life experiences. The instructional strategies and the EdTech implementations that are shared in this chapter have the potential to help lessen the reading comprehension deficit and make reading comprehension far more visible.

"Without an improvement in understanding texts, readers will continue to miss out on understanding important information. They will struggle in trying to incorporate critical and higher order thinking skills into their life experiences."

With an effect size of 0.59, direct instruction is a powerful way to introduce learners to new information and strategies. With the tremendous focus on identifying textual evidence in current educational learning standards, modeling study skills —especially text annotation through reading closely— demonstrates how to locate text evidence. Showing students how to apply Serravallo's (2015) strategies offers a balance to citing textual evidence, and allowing for a bit of personal connection and interpretation. By incorporating digital text access with various color options to highlight and annotate, students can refer back to their notes more readily to locate specific information. Furthermore, creating unique multimodal digital topic boards offers a chance for readers to connect with a text differently than if they were to merely write alphabetic notes on a piece of paper.

Moreover, many readers often prefer small group time over whole group instruction. It is more intimate when they can work with an educator at a teacher table to practice the new information that was modeled during a direct instruction lesson. What's more, they enjoy collaborating on previously learned strategies. And, they feel very "grown-up" when they have a job to do at an independent interactive video station. Not to mention, Hattie (2015) found effect sizes of 0.71 for spaced vs. mass practice and 0.52 for interactive video. For all of these reasons, amplifying a classroom with station rotation time and embedding spaced vs. mass practice in collaborative group compositions on Google Sites or a similar digital space is a win for everyone.

Finally, for struggling readers it often takes much repetition of a strategy for it to become something which they can apply independently. Often, when readers know the goal is to share their hard work with each other and other students, they tend to become more motivated. Book club discussions are something that can potentially take a lot of effort at the start. But, after students understand the expectations and practice successful conversing and note-taking, they enjoy preparing to produce their podcast episodes. As a result, the reciprocal teaching piece, with an effect size of 0.74, is a true culmination of implementing research-based reading comprehension strategies that are amplified with EdTech tools.

In closing, we read to create. All of the strategies and EdTech integration that have been presented in this chapter have implications for students of all levels across the world. When we offer opportunities for students to feel comfortable in understanding a text, they can create so much more. With high-quality direct instruction, time to read a variety of texts and develop reading strategies in a small group setting, and providing students with the tools to produce reviews and critiques, the learners of today will become thinkers and leaders for tomorrow.

Moreover, as the available variety of EdTech tools continues to expand, there will be far more options for educators to offer learning opportunities like these for their students. All of the examples in this chapter can be done with little to no cost, and there are user-friendly tutorials available for educators of any level. Educational practitioners around the globe can be assured that the growing body of tools and resources will enable them to integrate dynamic and amplified learning experiences for all students. And, even if you are just starting out, there are many resources available to guide you on your journey.

To get started with amplified learning in teaching reading

comprehension, pick one of these strategies and give it a try! If you aren't sure where to start, consider the direct instruction piece. Start by determining the desired reading comprehension learning outcome. Then, create a teacher account on www.readwork.org, www.newsela.com, or another similar tool (if you don't already have one) and start exploring texts that fit your students' interests and reading levels.

Select one text for your first lesson and read the text, noting places you want to pause to think aloud. Practice highlighting and annotating the text, so you are comfortable doing it live. You can also create a color-coded key to post near your screen. If you are curious about other features that are available, be sure to explore the myriad of tutorials that are posted for teachers and students. Then, simply gather your readers in class and explore the site together. Later, after you and your students are comfortable with the site, you can assign it during small group/station rotation time. Be sure to reflect on the experience so you can continue to grow the amplified learning experiences for your students.

EDITORS' CONCLUSION

Dr. Toney provides a stark reminder at the end of the chapter that we have a long way to go to help our students improve their reading proficiency. However, the bright spot of what she discussed is that there are a number of strategies we can integrate with technology to amplify our instruction and student learning. What stood out about this chapter is that there were about five strategies that can be implemented in classrooms fairly quickly. For example, digital anchor charts on interactive slides can be built and deployed from a learning management system within minutes. Additionally, this chapter discussed using a variety of tools to create multimodal opportunities for students to articulate the text's main ideas and key details will help students retain information and share what they learned with others. Recording podcasts is a great example of how students can use their voice instead of writing to discuss what a text is about as well as share what they were able to comprehend with their classmates. Last, a large emphasis was put on spaced vs. mass practice of reading, which is an essential learning strategy to build any skill we are trying to improve as learners. Specifically, Dr. Toney outlined how we should revisit reading concepts and skills taught earlier in the year throughout the year to practice those skills so students can retain those reading strategies.

Key Takeaways & Instructional Implications and Applications

- Asking and answering questions with the help of direct instruction, text annotation, and differentiated passages can help students comprehend the same story but at reading levels that meet the students' abilities.
- The Dig Deeper strategy can be used to help students understand main ideas and key details, which can be modeled and then integrated with Google Slides to give students an opportunity to compose those main ideas and key details on a multimodal platform that allows students to write, record, and hyperlink information.
- Reciprocal teaching can be integrated with podcasting tools to help students summarize, make connections, and share their insights with their classmates and school community.
- Digital anchor charts can be utilized as a topic board that can be provided to students with symbols and specific examples of the book they are studying. With digital sticky notes, they can invite students to express their thoughts in creative ways about the text they are reading.

ADDITIONAL EDTECH STRATEGIES FOR READING FROM EDUCATORS AROUND THE WORLD

Lisa Hockenberry - USA

Using Flip as a Tool to Build Reading Comprehension

Flip is such an amazing tool and with so many different ways to use it. I had students practice their reading fluency in Flip. Another way we used the tool in reading was to have students give book buzzes to classmates, which were quick summaries and previews of books in our library for our students. The ability to have students communicate and

connect with each other across the building and the world blew my kids minds.

This EdTech tool also allowed those who struggled expressing themselves in writing to be able to tell about their books they were reading. The students being able to create their book buzzes on Flip upped their engagement, and I was able to hear how well they comprehended a book. Students communicating about their book and commenting on each other's book buzzes allowed for interactions that do not always happen in a live classroom. The fun part is that we would put these QR codes in the front cover of books so students could scan it as they picked it out of our classroom library. It was always exciting to see when they discovered a QR code to watch a book buzz on the book they picked.

Flip enhanced our engagement in our classroom library and helped students bring books to life. Students would clamor over the books that had book buzzes on them because they couldn't wait to read the book and comment on the book buzz with their own take on the book. This was one of my most favorite ways to use Flip.

Kendall Strickler - USA

Facebook and the Global Read Aloud

Every year my third graders participate in the Global Read Aloud, an initiative started in 2010 by an educator in Europe. Participating teachers around the world read aloud a chosen book during the same six-week period and work to make connections with other classrooms around the world to share in the reading experience. Technology obviously plays a vital role in making these global connections.

The foundation for all the connections are found on Facebook. The Global Read Aloud has a main Facebook page, and then additional pages dedicated to each of the selected books, which vary by age level. These pages serve as a valuable resource for teachers and is where many of the global connections take root. You will see posts starting in the summer from teachers planning ahead and looking to make connections with other classes of the same grade level. Teachers look for connections that would be meaningful and new to their students, connections with students from around the world. I use Facebook to find my connections and will put out a post looking for teachers to connect with my class. Hundreds of teachers respond, as so many are eager for these global connections.

Once connections are established and the Global Read Aloud starts, one of my favorite platforms to amplify my teaching of reading during the

Global Read Aloud is Flip. It is a wonderful tool that easily connects my students to other readers. I use a Flip group where I have added other teachers as "co-pilots"; those teachers in turn add their students. My group from the 2021 Global Read Aloud had 466 members representing countries in North America, Europe, Asia, Australia, and Africa. As the "pilot" of the group, I pose questions eachweek about the chapters of the book we had all read, and students then respond. My favorite moment this year was when a student in my classwatched a response by a student in Kenya and declared, "She just explained that part of the book so well! I never thought of the characterthat way!" Boom. Reading amplified.

Padlet is another favorite tool. I created a Padlet group just for the book and invite all collaborating teachers to join. Similar to Flip, I pose a different question each week to which students respond. Sometimes it is a quick prediction question like, "What do you think will happen next?" or a character development question like, "How has the main character changed in the story?" Students love seeing how other kids around the world respond to the prompts. Similar to Flip, Padlet gives kids a chance to deepen their understanding of the book.

Elizabeth Jacobi - USA

Flip to Differentiate Reading Instruction

Flip has been a dynamic and engaging platform for students to respond to literature. Using response prompts via Flip has amplifiedmy teaching and encouraged children to share their thinking more organically. When my fourth graders use this tool, they are able to discuss their insights about characters and their traits as well as provide evidence directly from the text without being stymied by having to write out their thinking and the exact sentence or passage. This freedomto cite evidence directly from the text allows more opportunities for students to add support to their thinking and provides them more chances to read aloud and gain confidence reading aloud.

Flip allows for differentiation as well. Some students are able to explain more of their thinking verbally than through writing. Recording a reading response is a non-threatening way for readers who struggle with their handwriting, spelling, dyslexia, and/or dysgraphia to "show what they know". In addition, students who are shy about being on camera do not have to show their faces when they respond.

I will continue to use Flip because it is an excellent way for students to demonstrate their active reading skills, make predictions, and find connections as well as develop their critical thinking skills.

Chapter 2: Authentic Learning in Writing

By: Janet Ilko, Ed.D.

United States

"When you amplify the writing, you amplify the learning, and it starts with being a writer alongside your students." - Dr. Janet Ilko

WHY YOU SHOULD READ THIS CHAPTER

Writing instruction has taken on many new mediums as our society and schools have moved into the digital age. This can present many challenges as teaching writing can be difficult when modern classrooms have in-person and digital spaces. With this said, Dr. Ilko provides a personal and research-driven chapter on how to effectively teach writing in these environments by giving a number of strategies and EdTech integrations along with personal anecdotes of how to incorporate them within in-person and digital classroom spaces.

Throughout the chapter, several strategies are premised on empowering students and giving them a voice, through the writing process. Writing strategies are provided on editing, revision, and outlines are offered on how to amplify our student's voices by illustrating a few examples of spaces and mediums of how to do this in our digital classroom and school communities. These digital sharing spaces that can be used to share writing and student content discussed within this chapter include social media platforms, school web pages, and youth voices while the mediums of creating the writing include writing Tweets, incorporating writing within visuals posted on Instagram, and developing podcasts.

As you progress through the chapter, resources, and examples are provided on each strategy and integration outlined, which then can be utilized as a model for your classroom or school. Overall, there are a plethora of resources to help incorporate writing practices and amplify our student's voices. After reading this chapter, your writing toolbox kit will be ready to deploy these strategies and integrations within your classroom or school. Students will enjoy these new strategies and integrations as new forms of agency and content creation will be available to them to amplify their writing skills and, most importantly, their voice.

WRITING INSTRUCTION AMPLIFIED

When you amplify the writing, you amplify the learning, and it starts with being a writer alongside your students. I put myself out there right away, sharing my own writing process and drafts, because if you don't walk alongside your writers, they will not have faith in your practice. They will write for you, instead of growing into writers who develop and share their own ideas. Students tend to see writing as an end product for others, instead of one way to better understand themselves. As a classroom teacher and literacy coach, over the past three decades, I have seen firsthand the impact of technology in the classroom. From the first Apple 2E computer installed in my classroom, the onset of computer labs, then portable devices, access to the world through digital literacy changed the course of my writing instruction. Through my over a decade of work with the National Writing Project, the San Diego Area Writing Project, and my own research I have focused on the use of technology in empowering student voices, most recently in the middle and high school classroom. In this chapter, I will be sharing from our work together growing into digital producers and writers.

"When you amplify the writing, you amplify the learning, and it starts with being a writer alongside your students."

Noemi has been one of the students who has been part of

my digital writing journey. We met when she joined my class as a sophomore, and we spent the next two and half years together, growing as writers. Here, in Table 2.1, is an excerpt from my journal about that time, which I feel serves as the perfect introduction as to why we need to explicitly teach and support digital writing.

Table 2.1

A Digital Writing Journey

I met with a student the other day who reminded me of something critical; we need to be explicit in how we explain how things work in our classrooms. Noemi, a high school sophomore, and I have recently begun working together. She is a bright, articulate young lady, but she will be the first to tell you that school is not her thing. She struggles to complete her assignments and can feel overwhelmed sitting in a classroom full of students. She prefers to work alone and can easily be lost in the shuffle of a busy class because she appears to be actively engaged, when in fact, she has completed very little.

It was the end of the semester and students were pulling together writing pieces for their final portfolio. I noticed she had been sitting at her table for quite some time the day before, diligently working on the same assignment for the entire period.

I checked in with her periodically, asking, "What are you working on?"

"My essay," she replied, and it appeared as if she was. But at the end of the period, I pulled up her work discovering she had written about three sentences that entire hour. She didn't even seem frustrated, as I would have been as a writer who couldn't find words, but instead just quietly resigned to the fact that this is how writing worked. A long, laborious, and lonely process.

The next day she came back to class, and I convinced her to sit with me. I asked her to pull up her writing portfolio to see if we could find some samples in her writing over the semester to help with the essay. She hadn't completed almost any of the assignments, but instead bits and pieces of the many tasks completed throughout the quarter. I asked her why she hadn't finished many of her pieces, and she shrugged her shoulders and put her head down. "I don't know; I guess when I finally get started on something, we are moving on to something else. I always think I will come back to it, but I guess I haven't. When I look at everything I have to do, I just feel lost." I told her as a writer, sometimes we just need to pick a place to begin again. I suggested we start by revising the piece she was working on the day before because I thought what she had completed so far in the essay was well written and thoughtful. We sat down together and talked through the assignment. After a few clarifying questions, I realized what she needed was a frame, a scaffold on which to build her success and take on the work in bite-size pieces. She needed a way to navigate the work that made sense to her.

We spent about a half-hour reviewing the assignments, setting broad goals, and an outline. We then took this next step of letting her select where she began, on which assignment and broke that down even further. By the end of the session, she had accomplished more writing than she had in the previous two weeks. Why? Because as she put it, "Everyone tells me how behind I am, but no one showed me how to get out of it." It is as simple and complicated as that.

Noemi and I are an example of what teachers experience every day in trying to meet the challenges of teaching writing. Over the next few years, Noemi and I worked together as writers and grew and learned together navigating digital writing, becoming producers of digital media rather than simply consumers. Throughout this chapter, I will be sharing a number of strategies of how we became producers rather than consumers. The amount of time it takes to revise and produce quality writing can be overwhelming. But research demonstrates that writing solidifies learning. The processes involved in writing—searching for ideas, organizing, checking, revising, and so on—appear to be the processes through which thinking takes place (Bereiter & Scardamalia, 1987). Digital writing and the tools that allow students and teachers to write and revise in real-time can be game changers in how students produce writing and media, and in turn, share their learning and ideas with the world.

Working with Noemi and students like her has given me the impetus needed to use technology differently. Every student deserves the support and interaction that Noemi and I had, but time is always the challenge. However, integrating technology tools judiciously builds the scaffolds necessary to support targeted and meaningful instruction to help amplify our students' writing abilities. Therefore, this chapter will focus on four tools and strategies that build more time for meaningful writing instruction for both students and teachers.

"...integrating technology tools judiciously builds the scaffolds necessary to support targeted and meaningful instruction to help amplify our students' writing abilities."

THE RESEARCH & STRATEGIES

Online and blended learning and the subsequent challenges faced by teachers and students thrown into virtual instruction brought to the forefront the challenge of providing quality writing instruction. Evermnova (2020) and his research team remind us:

Writing with or without technology, writing is a complex process that requires students to brainstorm, plan, create, and revise their work. Exacerbating the need for effective writing instruction and technology integration are the significant writing needs of the students in today's diverse classrooms (Evmenova et al., 2020, 266).

Teachers are well aware of the power of the written word. When students can write about their learning, their understanding of the content increases. So why is it that writing instruction tends to take a back seat in not only content area classes, but in core English courses as well? Teachers know the importance and relevance of writing in their classes, but it tends to be something assigned and not explicitly taught. The use of digital tools and setting a real purpose for writing instruction fosters the motivation for both teachers and young writers who need to prioritize the time and effort needed to create quality writing instructional practices. Additionally, we want to not only ensure we prioritize time and effort, but we also want to provide opportunities for students to write with more intention and for teachers to give feedback more efficiently. Luckily, a number of strategies and tools can help us both accomplish these goals.

My work with the National Writing Project for over a decade has transformed my writing instruction, and the connection with these teacher researchers provides the research and access to best practices to support students. It is no surprise that they take the lead in research in both traditional and digital writing. In 2015, Troy Hicks and other National Writing Project fellows came together to research best practices in digital writing instruction. If we are to prepare our students for college and careers of the future, digital writing can no longer be just a place for students to publish an end product, but instead, it has the potential as a space to create, to collaborate, and to produce a variety of media beyond the black and white word.

"If we are to prepare our students for college and careers of the future, digital writing can no longer be just a place for students to publish an end product, but instead, it has the potential as a space to create, to collaborate, and to produce a variety of media beyond the black and white word."

Furthermore, we cannot allow our students to write in only one mode or modality. "Equipping students to write in only one mode traditionally on white paper in scripted genres will not serve students in their higher education experiences or in the workplaces of the future" (DeVoss et al., 2010, p. 5). By having students work with their contemporaries in network spaces, they will experience writing for broader audiences, writing in a wider range of genres, which will serve them well both in academic writing and their future careers.

The evolution of digital instruction, however, was slow. Teachers recognized the power of technology, but the impact of this type of instruction was minimal. Groups like the National Writing Project and the Pew Research Center surveyed instructional practices and studied many classrooms across the country in search of learning why the implementation of digital writing instruction was relatively slow. The findings were not surprising. Some 78% of the 2,462 advanced placement (AP) and National Writing Project (NWP) teachers surveyed by the Pew Research Center's Internet and American Life Project say digital tools such as the internet, social media, and cell phones "encourage student creativity and personal expression." In addition,

96% agree digital technologies allow students to share their work with a wider and more varied audience and it was found that 79% agree that these tools encourage greater collaboration among students. This research and subsequent work with my own young writers solidified my professional stance that relevance, student voice, and empowering student academic voice changes the trajectory of all students, but particularly those at risk of failing in our traditional classrooms.

In 2020, our educational system faced the greatest challenge in our history. With the onset of the COVID-19 pandemic, over 1.6 billion learners or over 94% of students in more than 200 countries faced school closures for extended periods of time (United Nations, 2020). The impact of social distancing and restrictive movement not only in schools but in our society forced educators to take a new stance on how we continue education during this crisis. Although the vaccine has allowed for a new re-opening of our cities and schools, the reopening and the continued uncertainty have far-reaching implications on our schools and instructional practices (Dhawan, 2020). Digital writing is no longer something taught in isolation due to these major changes in our schools and instruction but is now part of students' daily lives. Online, blended learning, and changes within traditional in-person classrooms have forced teachers to grow accustomed to digital writing and creating curriculum in digital spaces. As a collective profession, we have demanded internet access, digital tools, and digital curriculum to continue to provide an education to the millions of students in the United States who had to suddenly learn from home. Families and teachers have worked together like never before to navigate these challenging times. It has been an imperfect experiment, with many challenges. However, this is our opportunity to make real change in our educational programs. It is critical to involve our students and families in evaluating the digital tools we use in our programs. As digital development is a considerable part of the change, it becomes relevant to discuss whether all students have equal opportunities to take advantage of the possibilities offered. (Dahlstrom, H. 2019). As the world slowly returns to some sort of normalcy, the lessons taught over this past year cannot be lost. As a collective of great educators, now is the time to evaluate what works in our digital instruction, and what we can bring back to our practice as schools begin to slowly reopen.

Authenticity and purpose give both teachers and students the energy and grit to defy the odds as noted by teacher researchers in the National Writing Project. "Teachers, writing teachers especially, do not view good writing and the use of digital tools as being at war with each other," added Judy Buchanan, Deputy Director of the National Writing Project, and a co-author of the report. In fact, teachers who integrate writing throughout their curriculum seek opportunities to integrate digital tools to provide students the opportunity to practice real-world skills. "When educators have opportunities to integrate new technologies into teaching and learning, they are the most optimistic about the impact of digital tools on student writing and their value in teaching the art of writing. They gave countless examples of the creative ways they use emerging digital tools to impart writing skills to today's students" (Purcell et al., 2013, p. 1). But yet, this was still not the practice in most classrooms. Therefore, the goal of the remainder of this chapter is to illustrate how research-based instructional strategies can be utilized to illustrate how to teach writing within any classroom setting to amplify our students' writing.

Overall, with this scene set by the research and challenges of teaching writing, the purpose of this chapter and the following instructional integration and application vignettes is to create scaffolds teachers can use as a blueprint to create their own writing supports in their classroom. There are many strategies and tools teachers can select in creating a quality writing instructional program for students that develop student agency and teacher efficacy. This chapter will highlight three core elements of a quality writing program, effective feedback, harnessing social media, and the development and sharing of student portfolios. Table 2.2 illustrated on the next page highlights some of the research supporting the strategies selected that will be discussed within the vignettes of this chapter.

Table 2.2

Writing instructional strategies and EdTech integrations summarized

Instructional Strategy Theme	Research Proving Relevant Use of Technology in Writing Amplifies Student Learning	Strategies
Effective Digital Feedback Collaborative Commenting	Kittle (2008) Kinsella (2005) Kinsella and Feldman (2005) Henry, E., Hinshaw, R.,Al-Bataineh, A., & Bataineh, M. (2020)	Text Feedback Google Docs Voice Feedback Mote Collaborative Conferring Google Docs
Harnessing Social Media	DeVoss, D., National Writing Project, Eidman-Aadahl, E., & Hicks, T. (2010) Hicks, 2013	Twitter As Summary Writing Instagram Poetry
Student Portfolios	Purcell et al., 2011 Brooke, E. (2015)	Publishing on Public Spaces Digital Portfolios

STRATEGY INTEGRATION WITH EDTECH TOOLS AND INSTRUCTIONAL APPLICATION VIGNETTES

Just as writers set a purpose for their writing, the choice of tools in publishing and creating that work must also be purposeful. According to Henry et al. (2020), "teachers must ask themselves new questions when examining their pedagogical practices and the use of technology. When should digital tools be used? Will the use of digital tools simply offer another way of doing the same old thing? How should digital tools be used to enhance instruction? Teachers must carefully contemplate these questions and determine whether their pedagogical practices would be advanced using digital tools and whether these tools will amplify student learning."

Technology and Writing: Setting a Purpose for the Tool

There are two ways of thinking about using technology in the classroom with your students. The materials are either meant to be consumed by the learner or inspire the learner to produce media for others. In my experience in working with students, the balance of media use is weighted heavily on the side of student consumption. Many programs ask students to complete low-level cognitive tasks such as simple "cloze" activities, multiple-choice, or matching type questions after reading a text. Although there is a time and place for such interaction, in order to create digital spaces for students to develop their writing, the focus must promote student autonomy and create an environment centered around the learner. The potential for small group instruction and flipped learning formats provide students with extra support to access the content in relevant and timely ways. Students become directors of their own learning, empowered by the variety of digital supports and materials available. To create quality online programs for young writers, the tools we select must be driven by student interaction, so they become not only consumers of media but creators of media.

In thinking about how to select technology tools for the content classroom, planning is critical. Knowing your purpose for the technology you want to incorporate into the learning is essential to making the best selection for students. It is beyond the scope of this chapter to make specific selections, but there are important things to consider when looking at tech materials to support your content classroom. Working together with teachers, we use the following criteria in making decisions on what to integrate into our instructional practice (Brooke, 2015).

- Careful selection of technology tools that adapt to each student's abilities and needs
- Use instructional programs that capture student data and provide time and support for teachers to use that data in meaningful ways.
- Choose personalized learning technologies that allow teachers to provide recommendations for teacher interventions as students work through the program. In other words, teachers serve as a guide on the side, integrating the tools and selecting appropriate supports that enhance the course content.
- Select appropriate instructional resources that help the teacher to connect performance data to instructional strategies. The data should be easy

for teachers and students to access and provide meaningful feedback for specific goals.

When integrating technology, the focus of instruction for students should always be to provide more connections and opportunities to interact with peers and the teacher. Particularly for our English learners, technology can be an opportunity to build language and connection, but many times, students interact with programs that minimize the opportunity for student production of academic language. So many times, we see students working in isolation, "face in a screen," which defeats what we feel is the true potential in using technology to support language growth. Individualized instruction does not mean isolationism for our students. Going back to setting the vision and purpose of including technology support in your content and writing classes, the focus must always be on connection. Connection directly to the content, or connection to the teacher and peers in the classroom. For example, discussion boards can provide the spaces some of our quiet students need to think through their responses and add their reflections to class discussions when speaking even in a small group can feel overwhelming. It is the building of an academic community that will change how students view themselves as scholars and active participants in the classroom and their own learning.

Once we have established that understanding in our classroom community, students will begin to develop language, not as something that is merely an assignment, but hopefully something more intrinsically motivational. By getting to know our students, building relationships, and identifying their aspirations and goals gives us the connection we need as educators to bring relevance and meaning to our instruction and motivate our students to excel. Integrating technology into the writing process can build the scaffolds and support students' need to be successful communicators, and in turn build a stronger classroom community of learners.

Using Google Docs for Feedback and Conferring

When thinking about my initial work with Noemi highlighted in the introduction, those conversations happened face to face in a classroom over a span of a few weeks, which ultimately had the greatest impact on both her growth as a writer, and my growth as a writing teacher.

Researchers and teachers for decades know the value of conferring with students. By focusing not on the writing, but instead building a relationship and understanding of the goals and strengths of the writer. As Penny Kittle (2008) shares, "writers grow with regular response to their work and the work of other writers. Students need time to respond to each other about ideas" (p. 5). I wanted to ensure that I could have that same interaction with all my students in class, but how would that be possible given the constraints of time and the sheer number of students?

In the past year of toggling between various classroom settings, this connection became even more important. Suddenly we were no longer in the classroom together, so how could I possibly provide the support my writers would need? Sometimes the simplest tools yield the greatest results. My students all have access to Chromebooks and the Google Workspace platform. With basic keyboarding skills, students were able to share their documents with me, and revision suddenly became more accessible. Students being able to use the voice typing feature allowed hesitant writers to be able to get their thoughts on the page, a game-changer for many of my English learners and struggling writers. My ability to interact meaningfully by giving specific feedback, in real-time, provided easy documentation of our discussions and focus. Suddenly, the collaboration that was happening with students like Noemi could happen both synchronously and asynchronously. There are many great tools out there, and by the time this book goes to publication, there will be even more tools and extensions to try. Regardless of the tools we use, I have discovered three non-negotiables in supporting revision and writing instruction: text feedback, voice feedback, and collaborative commenting.

Text Feedback

One of the easiest ways to give student feedback is to use the commenting feature found in Google Docs. Many word documents include this feature, which allows teachers to provide students' feedback as well as opportunities for students to reply to their teacher's feedback. Illustrated below includes a step-by-step tutorial of how to add comments on Google Docs:

- **Select the text** you want to leave feedback for.
- Next click the **"Add a comment" button** that pops up to the right of the document.
- Or press **Ctrl-Alt-M** if you prefer keyboard shortcuts.
- Or click **"Insert"** then **"Comment"** in the top menu bar.

Once the comment box opens up, you can enter your text right in the comment box and leave your comment on the right side of the document. Not only can I leave text comments, but I can add hyperlinks to helpful videos or provide additional sources of mentor text for students to review. Students can also reply to the comments creating a visual conversation about the text. This is particularly helpful when students are working asynchronously, as they have feedback to review once they have left the classroom.

Once a comment is resolved, the writer can hide the comment by clicking "resolve" to hide it. The commenting feature also serves as revision documentation for student portfolios. By clicking the "Comments" button at the top of the screen, all the comments reappear on the page, providing both the writer and the teacher the opportunity to review changes made throughout the writing process.

Voice Feedback

Another option for revision is using voice feedback where you record your voice and attach that as a playable comment in the document. Many teachers and students prefer this method because using your own voice feels more personal. In many cases, it is also faster and easier than typing. My students who struggle with keyboarding appreciate this feature. I have been using Mote, which is an extension offered in Google Chrome's Extension Store. Like most extensions, there is a free and paid version. This extension allows you to leave voice comments and audio content to shared documents, assignments, emails, and forms. Mote is integrated into Google Docs, Slides, Sheets, Forms, Classroom, and Gmail. Students can also leave voice notes and react to your feedback and comments. This option builds oral language and provides a more personalized option to discuss the assignment. In distance learning, the connection of voice has been a game-changer in building community. To use the Mote extension tool for voice feedback, review and follow steps:

- Install the extension using the Chrome Web Store Link. Because this is a Chrome Extension you must be using Chrome on your PC, Mac, or Chromebook.

- Once you are in a Google Doc, highlight the text where you want to leave a comment and click add comment.
- Within the comment tab, you will see the Mote icon. Click on the icon and it will immediately begin recording your voice comment.
- When you are finished, click done. Immediately a pencil icon will display, and you can edit or revise your comment.
- Once you are satisfied with the comment, you can exit, and the recording will be there in the comment section for student review
- Students can also send a comment back to you by downloading the app on their device as well.

Figure 2.1

A QR code to learn more about the Mote extension

qrco.de/ampglobaledu51

Whatever tool you use to voice record, the impact of the personalization of the feedback is what is important here. Many students who may not speak out in class or on Zoom, will reply in this format. Therefore, I will illustrate how this occurred in my classroom by discussing how to use the feedback tool in real-time.

Using Voice Feedback in Real-Time. Kevin is a student that I coach in my English 3 class. He is not one who likes to revise and tends to be the one-and-done writer. If we were working together in class, or during a tutorial, he would revise his work. However, on his own, he often did not remember the feedback and would come back to class with no real changes. By leaving the oral comments, he was able to listen to the feedback, and then give me oral feedback as well. Our revision sessions became more effective because he was able to speak rather than type his responses, giving him faster response time, and an ability to focus on the work rather than the spelling and grammar that was sometimes a struggle. The focus was instead on content revision, which over time, he began to recognize that revision was not simply about editing, but instead, focusing on the message of the writing. To further illustrate this interaction with Kevin, a visual in Figure 2.2 is shown below that depicts the changes made due to the oral feedback using Mote.

Figure 2.2

Using Mote for voice feedback

Collaborative Commenting During the Writing Process

Student written comments and voice feedback can be utilized for student collaboration as well during the writing process. One of the best features of Google Docs is the collaboration feature. Students can use this feature to provide feedback and engage in the peer-review process. Teachers can use the collaboration feature to monitor students' progress. This tool facilitates teacher comments on student essays synchronously or asynchronously, which gives the teacher and student feedback throughout the entire writing process, building a powerful writing support system within the classroom. Here is a quick step-by-step overview of how this may work in your classroom using Google Docs.

1. Once a document is open in Google Docs, select the Share tab in the upper right-hand corner. Students can invite their writing buddy or buddies to be collaborators, by simply entering their email addresses and clicking "Invite Collaborators." When students sign in as a collaborator, it is important that they use their first and last name by clicking on the settings link on the doc page. This ensures you can easily identify revision partners and groups. Make sure they also invite you, the teacher, so that you can monitor their progress and provide feedback along the way.

2. After students are entered as collaborators and after they collaborate by commenting on each other's work, each collaborator will have a different color to distinguish what they contributed to the document. This color-coding is a great tool for the teacher in monitoring student participation in the revision process. By quickly reviewing the document you can easily note who is making comments and provide support as needed.

3. As your students revise a document, the revision screen will show who worked on the document and when they worked on it. When two students

edit an essay, you can easily see who did what by comparing two revisions or browsing through the revisions. Finally, after the revision is completed, students can print the final copy without the revisions appearing in the work. As the teacher, you can look through the revisions and note what changes were made by whom throughout the process before they submitted their final work.

The critical advantage is this tool allows for revisions throughout the writing process. So many times, I have had conferences with students who believe they are "one and done," and do not see the value of revision. Working on shared documents and having the ability to give meaningful feedback throughout the process makes the final products better, and more importantly, reinforces the process of writing over the product.

Modeling Quality Comments with Academic Language. One key element to making the revision process successful is modeling quality commenting. Like any type of writing or procedure, students must be explicitly taught how to comment effectively. All students, but particularly English Language Learners, may need models and frames to guide their responses. Students need to learn how to use academic language in their peer responses. Kate Kinsella is a prominent researcher on academic language and the impact of learning that language is a gateway to student success in both school and the workplace. Her work highlights English language learners but can be applied to all students in navigating learning in a virtual format.

According to Kinsella (2005), academic language can be defined as 1) the language used in the classroom and workplace, 2) the language of text, 3) the language of assessments, 4) the language of academic success and 5) the language of power. It is the combination of academic vocabulary and academic discourse. Academic vocabulary is defined as the vocabulary critical to understanding the concepts of the content taught in schools. Academic vocabulary includes content-related vocabulary and high-frequency academic words such as Bloom's verbs.

Academic discourse provides students with the language tools (i.e., vocabulary and syntax) necessary to competently discuss the topic using complete sentences. Structured dialogue in the form of "sentence stems" provides a scaffold for students to appropriate academic language in meaningful contexts (Kinsella & Feldman, 2005).

Much like building a sturdy wall, the academic language is the bricks, and the academic discourse is the mortar holding those terms together in a sound structural format. By providing students with sentence frames, you give them the structure they need to build their own academic voice, and raise the level of feedback by focusing the type of comments to be more content specific, and hopefully more valuable to the writer. Creating effective sentence frames requires the analysis of the academic language students need to complete their tasks effectively. The use and development of sentence frames and ensuring their availability both during synchronous and asynchronous instruction is ensured when the frames are built into the lesson slides and graphic organizers provided to students. Some of the frames we have used come from the sentence framework of Kate Kinsella; these are examples of frames used in an editorial writing unit (Kinsella, 2005).

Table 2.3

Language frames for editorial writing

Language of Justification	I believe this because... My primary reason for thinking so is... Perhaps the most convincing reason for this is...
Language of Persuasion	Based on the evidence presented so far, I believe that... Although some people claim that... Opponents argue that .... It is vital to consider... The advantages of_____outweigh the disadvantages of_____insofar as... The statistics are misleading because they do/do not show...

Although these supports are developed with the English learner in mind, these supports are offered to all students and highlighted in the instruction to help all students try them on as part of their development as writers. Be sure to always model where these language frames are located and refer to them within any mentor text utilized to model their incorporation within writing. Ultimately, this will help with students incorporating them into their writing.

Harnessing Social Media to Amplify Wiring and Student Voice

Harnessing social media is an effective tool to publish and motivate young writers. Using social media tools such as Instagram and Twitter connect students to the outside world. By creating a class account, you as the teacher can model effective digital safety strategies, responsible posting, and monitor the content that is published. It is important to review your site and district policy on social media use. Make sure you have permission to publish forms on all your students and follow all guidelines for posting pictures of your classroom and students. With that being said, do not shy away from these powerful tools. Social media can be a positive way to connect with other students and their families. I have both a Twitter and Instagram account that I use exclusively to showcase our classroom events and student work. Students post their work and give the world a glimpse into the work we do as writers in our classroom. Both Twitter and Instagram are wonderful tools for students to summarize and prioritize learning. Let me share two examples.

The Power of Twitter

Twitter is a wonderful tool to teach summary writing. Let's face it, students tend to struggle with writing summaries of their learning, and this is perhaps one of the most common tasks asked of students across content areas. Students tend to write down everything or write down next to nothing, focusing on the details, rather than synthesizing the information to come up with the main idea. It is a challenging skill that takes repetition and focus to master. Basically, when we summarize, we take on larger sections of text and reduce them to their most important elements. Summarizing is the first step in learning the more complex skill of synthesis. In synthesizing, the most important information is combined from multiple sources, requiring the reader to take the summary and add their own thoughts, experiences, and opinions to make connections and create their own new idea. Using Twitter is an excellent tool to force students to synthesize information.

By incorporating Twitter into your classroom routine, students have multiple, meaningful opportunities to practice synthesizing information and communicating effectively with others. Using the format found on Twitter, students are forced to get to the heart of their learning and strip away words and phrases until they have only the most important elements left. With only 280 characters in a tweet, students are forced to edit for clarity and impact. Examples include asking students to summarize a chapter using a tweet, or highlight key learnings from our lesson of the day and post on our classroom Twitter account.

For example, within my English Language Development (ELD) support classroom, teams of students were tasked with reading a pair of articles on global warming and the potential impact of the use of electric cars on the carbon footprint in California. This was a complex process, and Robert and his partner Liliana were struggling to find the main ideas. Here is an excerpt of several key facts Robert and Liliana gleaned from the articles:

Plug-in electric vehicles (EVs) can help keep your town and your world clean. In general, these cars produce fewer emissions that contribute to climate change and smog than conventional vehicles. There are two general categories of vehicle emissions: direct and life cycle. Life cycle emissions are created when people produce, process, distribute and use cars and fuel. Direct emissions come straight from the vehicle. They are emitted through the tailpipe, through evaporation from the fuel system, and during the fueling process. All electric vehicles produce zero emissions, with hybrid cars producing less emissions than cars that run strictly on gasoline.

In small groups, students were tasked with writing a tweet explaining their view on reducing emissions. This required students to highlight key terms and negotiate the terms in meaningful ways. Students using the word count tool on a Google Doc can check their character count as they revise their tweets. Working together, Robert and Liliana synthesized the key points to structure their tweet.

Table 2.3

Example of a tweet summarizing EV cars

Electric vehicles provide us with cleaner air by producing zero emissions. Cleaner air makes a better planet. Support EV cars in your community by supporting charging stations in your neighborhood. #everyemissioncounts

Sometimes less is more. In synthesizing key points in this way, there is rich high-level discussion in selecting what is deemed relevant to include in the tweet. The level of engagement is high, the discussion is focused, and students leave with a focused review of the information. Giving students multiple opportunities to synthesize the information provides the much-needed practice of this important and challenging skill.

A note from Becky: To engage students in a similar Twitter activity without having students create Twitter accounts, teachers can utilize Wakelet or Padlet. Through Wakelet, teachers can create a new collection with a prompt similar to a Twitter post, and each student group can respond to the prompt. Similar to Twitter, students can add emoticons to other's posts. With Padlet, students can add their synthesis (Twitter-like post) to a Padlet board and respond to one another or add "likes" to posts.

Visual Windows to Writing through Instagram

Instagram has been predominantly used as a visual window into our classroom. We post photos of class events, quotes from student work, and photos generated by some of the students. But, Instagram can be more than just cute puppy photos, it is an opportunity to engage students in writing short powerful text pieces, improving both their literacy and literacy media skills. Instagram is full of creative writing opportunities if you just know where to look.

Just this past year, as I was trying to find ways to motivate my students to read and write poetry. I was scrolling Instagram and found a beautiful poem carefully posted on an image in my feed @atticuspoetry. Soon I was hooked and began to look for other poets. I found a new genre, Instapoetry. Instapoetry is defined as short, free verse poems that are often paired with a drawing or shared on an image that represents the poem. Many poetry critics do not take this genre of poetry seriously, but I feel this is an amazing mentor text opportunity for students to dabble in poetry and publishing.

In honor of National Poetry Month, we added this new poetry genre to our readings, and many of my students were hooked. To create an instapoem, the work is not only about the writing but using visual images to suit the poem. Students studied a variety of instapoets both for their poetry structure and image selection. We used the tool Canva.com to create posts using stock photos or images we created ourselves. This is a free site that provides images and formatting for a variety of social media formats. Students are motivated to publish on this site because they can create professional looking pieces easily. There is a lot of flexibility in the design element and all images are cleared for public domain use.

One way to publish these instapoems is through a webstory. Web stories combine a few simple panels to tell a story or highlight writing. Depicted in Figure 2.3, National Writing Project fellow, Anna Maine, created this short video using Web Story Creation, which is on how to create web stories on the youthvoices.live (Maine, 2021).

Figure 2.4

QR code to learn more about how to create web stories on youth voices

qrco.de/ampglobaledu53

Another way to publish poetry is through the use of web story tools. After reading a variety of short poems, Julia decided to create her own Let Me Bring A Light poem, which is depicted in Figure 2.5.

Figure 2.5

A QR code to a Let Me Bring a Light poem

qrco.de/ampglobaledu54

Flash forward to Noemi two years later. She has discovered that she loves poetry, and graphic novels, and is interested in media arts. Figure 2.6 can take you to view Noemi's poem Paint Me Like I Am.

Figure 2.6

A QR code to Noemi's poem Paint Me Like I Am.

qrco.de/ampglobaledu55

Overall, the use of digital support over the past two years changed both Noemi and me as writers and publishers. This example is my reminder of the potential of digital writing and media creation, which can be shared with the world.

A note from Becky: For younger students to create instapoems, I recommend utilizing Google Slides or PowerPoint. The slide deck template can be set up for each student to have their own slide. Students can find pictures online or create their own on their individual slide. Having a class slide deck allows students to see each other's instapoems for inspiration.

Creating a Podcast to Amplify Student Voice - This I Believe

How can we create positive and powerful civic engagement opportunities for our students? Writing should not just be confined to assignments within the four walls of the classroom. In order to promote collaboration, academic discourse, and relevance for students, I had students create digital podcasts and videos about self-selected topics of interest. Using the curriculum from sites like KQED, NPR, This I Believe, and TED-Ed programs students created a variety of podcasts about their ideas and beliefs on issues facing our country today. The students wrote across content areas, used a variety of academic language supports, and most importantly shared their voices with others on global issues. By creating a platform where students could share their thoughts and ideas with a broader audience, we provided motivation, relevance, and rigor that helped our students recognize the power of voice and sharing knowledge in the broader community.

Teaching students to navigate information online, through images, video, and articles not only provides the visual scaffold that students need but teaches real-world skills that can be applied to a variety of situations. Integrating the multimedia effect of technology takes away the "teacher-centered" pattern of instruction. Students have the opportunity to become more self-directed and inevitably build more time for conversation and learning when students are partners in the learning. This led to the creation of podcasts.

One of the biggest challenges for my own teaching is the tech learning curve. I am not extremely techy! I have dabbled in the digital writing arena for the past ten years and this statement is still true. I know enough to get started, and I trust my students enough to learn together. It is not about the tool, but instead, it is about amplifying student voice. I think of what I want my students to do, and then I seek people with more technology knowledge than me to guide me in how to make that happen. I have a lot of personal tutoring to do each time I start a new project. I have created podcasts with my students for several years.

The reason podcasts are such a great project is the focus

on student voice. Thinking about prosody, the tone, speed, and volume of our speech gave light to the content and their words, rather than the bells and whistles of video media. This type of production is interesting to me because it relies solely on student voice and a little background music. The focus is truly on voice, both in the sense of content, and the actual voice that so many students do not want to share out loud. This idea of actually speaking their words, without the bells and whistles of video or photography is a serious challenge. Students were very nervous, to the point where I opened my classroom up before school, after school, and during lunch so they could "privately" record. They re-recorded their work at least ten times before they finally published it. Thank you, Troy Hicks, for your inspiration and your chapter on crafting audio texts in your book *Crafting Digital Writing, Composing Texts Across Media and Genre* (Hicks, 2013, 88). By reviewing this book, you will find many resources to support this work.

Now, some people would wonder why I would give up two weeks of class periods to complete such an "old school" podcast. It is simple, my kids need to learn to revise. They also need to learn how to speak in front of others. Most of my leadership class population consisted of English Learners. They reclassified and no longer required ELD class, but every middle school student needs help with oral language production for an academic purpose. Middle schoolers will talk a mile a minute until you ask them to speak in front of an entire group, and then you can hear the crickets chirp through the deafening silence.

My leadership class consisted of students who found school relatively easy. The average grade point average was above 3.5 (on a 4.0 scale), and they would coast through some of their classes because they did not feel overly challenged. Many did not see a need to improve or revise, and it had been a challenge to prepare them for the very real changes that they will be facing with these new common core assessments and life in high school and beyond. Ultimately, they needed to learn how to struggle, and improve, and feel a little uncomfortable. This is the perfect project to challenge students to produce more than they think they can.

A note from Becky: Flip is a great alternative to student podcasting and recording and is accessible to all grade levels (including early elementary). Through Flip, teachers can determine the maximum amount of time for students to record along with the added features available for students. While many podcasting tools can be utilized for older students, younger students may benefit from starting with Flip and working up to podcasting. An example of one such podcast is called the 4th Grade Innovators Podcast by fourth grade teacher Zach Rondot and his students.

Curating Student Work

As a teacher, I struggle and feel uncomfortable trying to figure out how to record, save, post, and publish student work. I constantly feel challenged in this arena. I will illustrate a few of the questions I have pondered as I rework and revise developing digital writing projects, including podcast lessons for students.

1. What program will work on our "old technology," and will it transfer to the newer version?
2. What can I share on my blog, our school website? Will I need to modify the format?
3. Where do the podcasts go once I upload them to iTunes? (I lost them for a little while.) Is my new computer going to take the podcasts from the older versions of our class laptops?
4. Is there an additional permission form needed? Oh God, tell me our current forms cover this, or do I need another letter to publish on "This I Believe"... damn attorneys.
5. How can I set up my classroom so that students can record in relative silence? (Not possible hence the extended opportunities for students to come in on their own time.)

These questions still ring true for any teacher taking on digital writing projects. They are messy and time-consuming.

They are also powerful, and I would venture to say life-changing for the student writers and the classroom climate.

Flash forward to this past year. I had my high school students complete a similar task. We now have many options for podcast publishing. We can record ourselves using Google Voice and upload it. We also used Vocaroo.com as an option. Students can use their cell phones to record and upload those as well. My point is, it isn't about the tool, but the purpose. The importance of a podcast is to have students write and revise pieces that are important to them. The value is sharing the message. The power is the practice and revision it takes to clearly articulate that vision. Podcasts are just as relevant today as they were seven years ago when I first experimented with them. Figure 1.6 will take you to a student's podcast on self-image. When listening, I guarantee you will hear this student's story and voice and feel changed after listening to it.

A note from Matt: There are a number of free podcasting recording tools, which include Anchor and Audacity. Additionally, several platforms such as Podbean, Spotify, and Buzzsprouts are freemium platforms to host podcasts once created. Then, teachers can utilize Google Sites, WordPress, or Weebly as free sites to use as a landing platform to compile and curate the student-created podcasts.

Figure 2.7

A QR code to a student-created podcast on self-image

qrco.de/ampglobaledu56

Make Students' Work Visible - Public Digital Portfolios

Once students are comfortable writing and producing media in digital classroom spaces, there are many opportunities for students to share their work more broadly. According to teachers, students' exposure to a broader audience for their work and more feedback from peers encourages greater student investment in what they write and in the writing process as a whole (Purcell et al., 2013, p. 1). There is nothing more impactful on student writing than generating audience and purpose, and digital spaces for students and teens do just that. In my own experience in blogging and publishing with students, teaching digital citizenship and cyber safety is critical to the success of the project. Transparency and communication with families is the first step to creating a safe and powerful on-line portfolio.

Common Sense Media, a non-profit organization founded

by Jim Steyer in 2003 provides education and advocacy to families and educators to promote safe technology and media for children. Bill Fitzgerald (2016), Director of Privacy Initiative at Common Sense Media, suggests the following when sharing student work online:

> If you are going to share student images and work on social media, make intentional choices about what you share, how you share, and why you share. Additionally, ask your district about more granular policies for parents and learners. While the initial change might be hard, over time the more flexible rules will make your work easier, and increase trust between you, your students, and their guardians.

Every school and district will have its own policies on publishing in public spaces. It is important that you review and follow those policies as you move toward a more public sharing of student work. Many teachers shy away from broader publication, but if 2020 has taught us nothing else as educators, it is that it is possible to connect from virtually anywhere. Our classroom has grown, and our breadth and depth of producing and sharing student writing should continue to grow as well.

A note from Matt: Digital portfolios are powerful ways for students to display their skills over time. They can be utilized for any subject or skill a student is learning. A number of platforms for digital portfolios include Wakelet, Google Sites, WordPress, Canva, and Weebly. Digital portfolios can be long-lasting content artifacts for our students. When working in tandem with other teachers, digital portfolios can be great alternatives to traditional grades to demonstrate proficiency. Last, they provide opportunities for student's voice and personalization to shine, which can create student agency, empowerment, and engagement in school.

Over time, I have become an advocate for student publications on a broader scale. Why? Because writing for a broader audience gives students relevance and a need to revise. You make it better because you get feedback from others, and not writing in a vacuum. But first, students must feel comfortable sharing in your classroom space. You must create a learning environment that is inclusive and safe, so students feel they can take risks. They must know that they can and will make mistakes, and those mistakes make for better writing and opportunities for revision. Start small with writing groups and an author's chair. Provide frequent opportunities for students to share their writing, not just the final project, but highlighting their work throughout the process. As discussed earlier in the chapter, shared documents are a great first step to growing the audience. Having students share breakout rooms is another great way to bring author's circles to our virtual environment. Again, building trust in small steps, and modeling that risk-taking by reading your own imperfect writing brings a level of trust and comfort to the classroom.

Another step to sharing your work more broadly may be as simple as facilitating partnerships with other classrooms or periods of students on your own site. Creating a classroom blog or publishing site using templates like WordPress or Edublog allows you to control the audience and space. Going back to your classroom social media is another small step in publishing publicly, posting student work links on your class Twitter or Instagram accounts.

Last, we have started a writing club on our campus, and interested students have come to our digital space to create and share their self-published writing. We currently are part of a teen publishing site youthvoices.live through the National Writing Project. This is a youth-powered social network and multimedia publishing platform that was started in 2003 by a group of teachers from across the country through their local writing project sites. The purpose is to connect students to read and write about their own passions, to connect with other students, and to share knowledge. Youth Voices is a platform for youth to write about their interests, both in school and outside of school: what they are reading, what their hobbies or future careers might be, what they enjoy in their spare time. Like all of us, students follow our national leadership and form opinions. They are also welcomed to write about those topics as well. The HSHMC Youth Voices Page is a culmination of several years of students at my current high school taking that next step to share with other teen writers. It has been a powerful platform and support in working with students in public writing spaces.

In sum, there are several sites for student writing publication. Large or small, it is important to broaden the audience for your students. Building a broader connection enhances not only student writing, but your own professional development as a teacher of writing. However, you start, I urge you to find small ways to bring your students' writing to the public view.

CONCLUSION - WRITING INSTRUCTION AMPLIFIED

In teaching young people to write, guiding them to discover their own reflections on their process is powerful. For example, Rowand Abraham, a sixth-grade student wrote: "You don't have to be the star, you just have to be the light shining on them," when asked about how we should best support each other in being writers. That quote has stayed with me over a decade later. When I remind myself of my role as a writing teacher, our job is to shine a light on what is possible both for our students and our profession.

"It is not solely about the writing structure, but it is always about empowering the writer."

In thinking about writing instruction through the years, one thing rings true, it isn't about the tool, it is about the process. It is not solely about the writing structure, but it is always about empowering the writer. As you think about planning your own instructional program, begin with creating something that meets the needs of the students in your room. Always start with the following questions to ask yourself:

- Who are they?
- What are their interests?
- How can you harness your existing technology and tools to best foster student engagement?
- If it is a new tool or app, how will I effectively incorporate it into my teaching and why?
- What will we need to learn and how will we grow together as a writing community?
- Who can I connect with to support my goals?

There is great power in teachers working together to harness the tools of the moment and expand your thinking of what is possible. Teachers need to share the wonderful things that happen each and every day in the classroom. We are more than media soundbites, and the work is wonderful, powerful, and ongoing. When you can, find a group of like-minded teachers, on your campus or in virtual spaces. Remember using Twitter and Instagram is a great way to start building your professional learning community. Find spaces like Youth Voices that fit your needs and skill sets. As teacher leaders, we must take the lead in this digital learning arena. There is power in teaching our students to be positive digital citizens, and to create media, not be defined by it. Giving students voice and choice gives space for students of all ages to try out their ideas, to communicate with each other, and to live in a digital world bigger than our classroom. It is messy, but worth the effort.

EDITORS' CONCLUSION

Writing is a means of creating content and sharing information with others in our digital age. Writing and synthesizing engaging content is key for being successful in the twenty-first-century. As a result, this chapter exemplifies a framework of strategies to help teach writing within our ever-changing classroom spaces within schools and how to empower our students by providing a number of different mediums to share their writing content and produce it.

After reading Dr. Ilko's personal experiences of teaching writing and examples of her doing it, it provides a key lens into how to teach writing in any setting and for any age.

Therefore, we suggest reviewing each strategy and examples of the work products created as a result of her collaboration with her students. With these strategies and EdTech integrations in your toolkit, we hope they empower you to incorporate them into your instruction one step at a time. Additionally, we highly recommend sharing the student's work with others within the school community. This will further empower the students as well as spread what you are doing in your classrooms to others in your building, district, and professional learning community.

Key Takeaways & Instructional Implications and Applications

- Feedback for writing is critical. Whether written or verbal feedback, it is essential students receive feedback and then do something with it. Also, collaborative feedback in the form of revisions/edits is another effective way to develop writing over time as well as in a collaborative way.
- Writing is a personalized skill that now can be integrated into a wide range of mediums such as summarized Tweets, visuals for social media, and podcasts.
- There are many places we can showcase student writing to develop further dialogue on a piece of writing or created content or house as a digital artifact demonstrating a skill and/or concept they have mastered. Digital portfolios are also great spaces to illustrate personalized learning as well as student agency.
- Modeling writing and using academic language sentence frames helps students formulate their writing.
- As a teacher of writing, ask yourself a number of questions to help you develop your lessons that best meet your student's needs such as who they are, what are their interests, how can we learn

together as a community, and how we can connect our students with tools that can foster engagement and meet our goals.

ADDITIONAL EDTECH STRATEGIES FOR STUDENT ENGAGEMENT FROM EDUCATORS AROUND THE WORLD

Additional EdTech Strategies for Student Engagement from Educators Around the World	
 **Professor Rebecca Cooney - USA**	**Google Drive & The Pivot Teaching Model** Google Drive is a free cloud storage service designed so users can store up to 15GB of files, photos, videos, pdfs, etc. It allows users to upload existing files and create content in Google Docs, Google Sheets, Google Slides, and more. Google Drive is accessible on PC and Mac platforms via desktop and mobile devices. Files, folders, and subfolders can be created and shared with others with view and edit access (Gildred, 2018). Before March 2020 and the dawn of the pandemic, I, like many instructors, had limited experience teaching and leading live, virtual, synchronous class sessions. Experience designing and delivering 100% online, asynchronous content was moderately useful—but overall, teaching remotely was an entirely new landscape. What was once done with ease in the face-to-face classroom now had to be re-imaged and redesigned for virtual delivery. In response to this challenge, I

immediately drew upon my knowledge and experience using collaborative tools in Google Drive including Sheets, Docs, Slides, Forms, and Jamboard to convert activities once accomplished through paper and whiteboards was replaced with interactive, collaborative tools designed to engage students, gel teams, and enlighten the learning process through technology and innovation. Through the use of online chat, breakout rooms, digital whiteboards, and online forms, students are allowed to connect from afar, communicate in real-time, and learn by doing. In preparation for the return to face-to-face teaching, I realized the immense value of this digital collaboration while also appreciating the reality that at any point, we may need to shift gears quickly and return to virtual, synchronous delivery. Thus, the "Pivot Teaching Model" was born. Using a combination of Canvas as our learning management tool, Google Sites as a vehicle for sharing in-class content and activities, and the Google Suite of tools for class session slides and collaborative in-class activities, I have successfully designed and implemented a new way of teaching that positions me to pivot at any point. I can teach this same content in-person or virtually with limited interruption and disruption to students and teams. The students are oriented, trained, and fully adapted to the model. They know where to find materials, how to reach me, and how to engage with each other regardless of the modality.

The Pivot Teaching Model includes the following components:

1) Learning management tool (e.g., Canvas) to store all of the fundamental course content including but not limited to syllabus and course schedule, assignments with rubrics, modules, quizzes, weekly announcements, discussion forums, lecture slides or recordings, access to course materials (e.g., textbooks or library), and attendance.

2) Google Site for live class sessions that houses content such as session lectures, in-class activities, team links, and examples.

3) Google Drive folder to house Google Slides (in-person class lecture decks), interactive activities created with Google Slides, Docs, Sheets, Forms, and Jamboard.

4) Optional…

a. Music! Spotify account with a class-created album.

b. More collaboration! Slack workspace for real-time communication through DMs, instructor Twitter feed, and channels for professional development, networking, Covid updates, and general non-course-related announcements.

Jennifer Ingold - USA

Increasing Historical Thinking and Reading Comprehension for All Learners Using Google Jamboard

Dissecting historical sources can amplify both historical literacy and reading comprehension. With Google Jamboard, teachers can create interactive learning experiences that will entice, enthrall, and engage all learners creating better understanding of and interaction with historical sources. As a virtual teacher, I created *The Debating and Debunking Historical Documents Series* using Google Jamboard in response to the needs of my diverse learning population. But the real magic has continued using these practices to transition back to in-person learning. This same strategy can be utilized as a segway to generate meaningful classroom conversation. To start, documents are uploaded onto Google Jamboard. Next, with one quick click, teachers can add text-filled "Sticky Notes" providing students with valuable direction and reinforcement on how to continue historical thinking practices to help them further analyze the sources they have been given. Student focus is reinforced with use of self-questioning techniques found on my authentic Enduring Issues Reference Table: $S1 + SB2 + DPM = EI$. Translated, *"What do I see? Who or what is the source? What is the deeper meaning?"* Then, based on the information presented, students

are asked to evaluate *"What possible enduring issues does this*

document bring up for discussion?" Students then record their own

responses on separate "Sticky notes" that are provided.

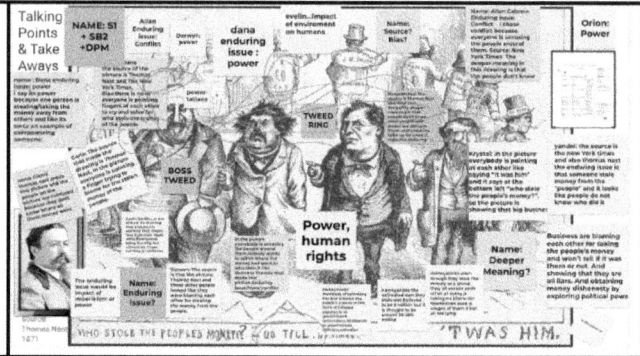

Courtesy of: J. Ingold, Authentic materials, "Debating and Debunking the Progressive Era" Google Jamboard Student Responses 4 February 2021

The sticky note feature on Jamboard provides a platform for helping all

students to launch into and lead larger historical conversations.

Research supports the idea that visuals and repetition are key strategies

to helping not just multilingual learners, but also for special education

students to be more successful in mainstream classes. When students

can verbalize, they are able to better understand and evaluate each piece

of evidence presented by their classmates. This adds greater

opportunity for all students to be able to participate in the conversation, making content even more easily accessible and comprehensive. Whether in-person or virtual, adding the extra layer of EdTech dimension with Google Jamboard can increase the quality of teacher-guided instruction. Google Jamboard's formative flexibility provides greater opportunity for every student's learning experience generating deeper understanding. Ultimately, every student deserves a chance to become more invested in their own learning. Google Jamboard can provide a map helping all students to better understand and identify with the issues surrounding the bigger picture of classroom instruction.

Trevor Aleo - *USA*

Storyboards and Essay Maps with Google Jamboard

Taking inspiration from Angela Stockman's work around #MakeWriting, I use Google Jamboard as a tool to help students create "storyboards" and "essay maps" as a pre-writing strategy. One of the biggest problems writing teachers face is finding ways to support students' ability to organize their compositions without over-scaffolding. If we simply provide students with a template, we prevent them from building conceptual understanding of text structures. However, if we don't provide tools that can help them to plan their organization, it often becomes an afterthought. Jamboard is the perfect EdTech tool for helping students develop an agile set of skills they can employ to organize their writing.

Students use the sticky notes as a way to chunk their ideas, visualize text structures, and pre-plan their writing. It's a form of rapid prototyping that allows them to explore and tinker with organizational structures. Visuospatial reasoning is one of the most powerful tools humans have at our disposal to represent complex relationships between ideas and Jamboard is the perfect tool to do exactly that.

Better still, this metacognitive process eventually becomes a skillset students use independently. Of all the strategies I teach my classes, this is the one that most often sticks with them. Every year I have students share how they use essay mapping in other classes to organize their thinking and writing.

Chapter 3: Authentic Learning in Mathematics

By: Sammy White

United Kingdom

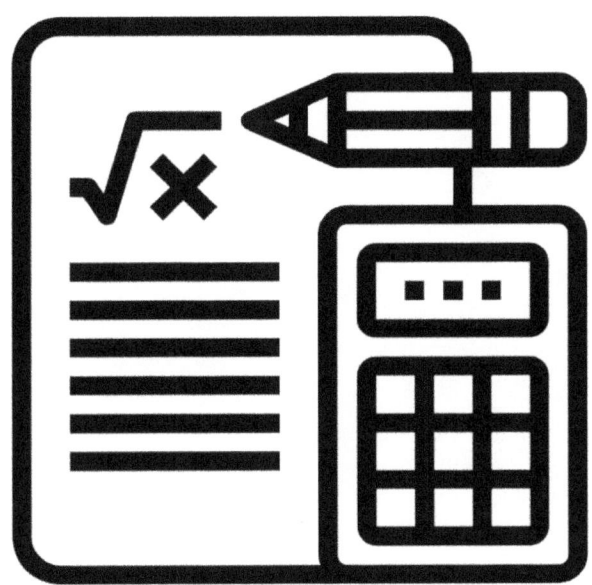

"The ability to explain how or why something is as stated can be derived from the formation of solid arguments in mathematics." - Sammy White

WHY YOU SHOULD READ THIS CHAPTER

Mathematics can be perceived as a challenging subject for many students. However, what this chapter provides is a number of strategies to help build students' self-confidence in mathematics to help them improve during formative and summative assessments. With many countries around the world that have high-stakes summative assessments, creating that self-confidence among students to do well not only helps their overall scores and what they learn but also their social-emotional well-being. The research-based instructional strategies within this chapter are linked directly to modeling and retrieval practice. Much of the conversation in regard to instructional strategies focuses on repeated practice and practicing correctly through the use of modeling to demonstrate the right solutions. If you are a fan of Daniel Willingham's cognitive science research, this will be right up your alley.

For the instructional EdTech integration vignettes, Ms. White provides a number of integrations to help facilitate modeling and retrieval practice. She outlines how to incorporate interactive videos into your instruction along with utilizing GIFs to create representations of how math problems are solved in bite-sized sequences. Additionally, she provides numerous examples of how Quizlet can be deployed to help students practice concepts and skills in preparation for assessment. Last, there is a focus on developing graphic organizers and practice assessments utilizing a wide range of online resources to provide opportunities for students to practice concepts and skills to help build their confidence and receive feedback in preparation for high-stakes assessments.

AUTHENTIC LEARNING IN MATHEMATICS

Mathematics can often appear as an abstract concept. The definitive yes or no answer is always said to be the aim. Yet, mathematics holds power for students, and effective teaching broadens student knowledge in many areas, not just mathematics. The ability to explain how or why something is as stated can be derived from the formation of solid arguments in mathematics. The skill of reasoning via logical arguments that are required for all subjects is developed firmly in the study of mathematics. The challenge mathematics teachers face is making mathematics accessible for all but not oversimplifying and creating linear processes for students to follow. It is the development of the rich understanding of the how and the why of mathematics that develops students' knowledge most (Chambers, 2010).

"The ability to explain how or why something is as stated can be derived from the formation of solid arguments in mathematics."

Mathematics teachers are challenged with making mathematics seem real and come alive. Visually representing problems that may be abstract in concept and bringing them to life. Writing mathematics effectively while using technology has proved challenging for years. Equation editors exist within traditional word processing tools, for example, Microsoft Word. Mathematics teachers have also made use of formatting tools, such as superscript, to enable mathematics to be written in text documents. Although these equation editors exist, they have often been complex for teachers and students to navigate. The challenge for the teacher is to create a carefully constructed question and example that can be readily shared. Once the teacher has navigated the existing equation editor and toggled between superscripts, the work can be shared. However, for students to be able to answer these mathematical questions, they too need training in how to add mathematics to their answers. In a traditional face-to-face format, this can be a challenge. Students need to be taught the correct format for writing the algebraic "x," for example. When we move to an online or blended learning environment, this becomes particularly difficult. The lengthy process that teachers have gone through to create work in a word processor must now be replicated by students in their answers.

A note from Becky: EquatIO is a commonly used equation editor in the elementary and secondary setting. With EquatIO's Chrome extension, educators and students can create, solve, and think aloud while utilizing math equations in Google Docs, Google Slides, and Google Forms. If EquatIO is not available, utilizing collaborative whiteboards allows students to write out and solve formulas in a virtual platform.

General Certificate of Secondary Education (GCSE) is the United Kingdom's (UK) qualification students are required to take when they leave high school. This is a two-year qualification that students begin at the age of fifteen. The current law is that, if students fail to achieve a grade of four in their GCSE mathematics exam they must continue to study the same qualification until they achieve grade four or turn eighteen, whichever happens earliest. The challenge for the mathematics teacher is to continue to cover content in readiness for this linear exam while ensuring that content taught over the previous two years can be retrieved also.

When teaching GCSE mathematics, poor retrieval of previous concepts and skills by students can often be diagnosed. For example, it is common to see students successfully attempt solving linear equations in class after a modeled example by the teacher. Yet the following semester the same students when beginning a unit on a more complex topic like solving linear equations, can display poor retrieval and need to recover the previous semester's topic again. Overall, this chapter will highlight research applied to teaching in a mathematics context to help amplify our math instruction. These research-informed strategies will be discussed and integrated with education technology tools that can be utilized to support student learning in mathematics.

THE RESEARCH & STRATEGIES

When thinking of the example highlighted above, when discussing the retrieval of solving linear equations, it is evident that the retention of the skill has become lost over time. Ultimately, much of the research of the strategies discussed in this chapter is centered around the

theme of the "critical goal of a classroom education is learning and retention of cognitive skills" (Roediger et al., 2011, p. 1). The strategy of adopting retrieval practice in teaching mathematics can lead to increased student retention of key mathematical concepts. In adopting the strategy of retrieval practice the teacher seeks to develop student retention of skills and knowledge learned in the classroom. Rather than leaving topics as covered and moving onto new units, previously taught topics are retrieved and assessed in low-stakes formative assessments. The process of retrieving the previously taught knowledge is learning in itself and creating an authentic learning experience for the students (Karpicke & Blunt, 2011). Frequently cramming before a test or re-reading material is often seen by students as a revision technique that will have a positive impact on their outcomes. A better-suited method to retrieval practice is low-stakes quizzing over time which can yield higher retention results for students. Studies show that test anxiety is not increased if quizzes are low-stakes and active for learners (Roediger et al., 2011).

A note from Matt: As discussed in Chapter 3, we live in the age of formative assessment. For us to measure where our students are now and to help us guide our instruction, low-stakes formative assessments are essential.

Additionally, we can use these assessments as a benchmark to help determine if our students have achieved learning goals, objectives, and standards during that given point in time when the assessment was taken.

Assessment through Quizzing to Build Retention

Low-stakes quizzing, also known as formative assessment, covers previously taught topics by providing opportunities for retrieval practice in the classroom. Multiple choice quizzes allow students to eliminate incorrect answers and construct logical arguments as to why their answer is correct. This self-explanation from students holds a high impact in classrooms.

Self-explanation and elaborative interrogation by students allow students to explain why a fact is true. Studies have shown in mathematics problem-solving examples for student retention of information and application of knowledge are greater when self-explanation and elaborative interrogation are used. Modeled worked examples by expert teachers that students can elaborate on and interrogate will have a high impact on student outcomes. (Dunlosky et al., 2013; Roediger et al., 2011).

 *A note from Becky: A great growth-mindset game to play with students is called "My Favorite No!" After taking a low-stakes quiz, the teacher sorts the correct and incorrect answers. Questions, one at a time, with an incorrect answer, are shown to the class and the students share what they notice. Then the teacher asks students to look for where the mistake was made and how to correct the mistake. Names are not attached to the incorrect answer, and the focus remains on building a growth mindset as a whole class.*

Modeling

Modeling by the expert teacher is a cornerstone of effective teaching. The expert teacher models the method they adopt to support students. Modeling lightens the cognitive load for students and allows them to observe an expert's approach and take on alternative approaches and ideas (EEF, 2018). According to Chambers (2010), "being able to see a series of mathematical steps gives pupils a sense of security and a feeling that they can tackle the expected work." When learning out of the classroom students can be supported by worked examples giving them the courage to tackle their independent work. Students feel supported by the teacher and can see the scaffolded steps the teacher has taken in tackling the problem (Chambers, 2010).

Repeated Quizzing to Practice Retrieval Practice

Students in UK secondary schools study to achieve GCSE certificates in their subjects. Repeated testing in mathematics is often included in many schools. Informal end of topic tests and more formal tests allow the teacher to gain insight into the strengths of students and areas to focus on in upcoming lessons. Testing increases anxiety for students. Mathematics students may already be experiencing anxiety due to the subject itself. Students may experience a dislike or struggle to access mathematics as a taught subject due to their anxieties (Hattie, 2009).

Researchers Pan and Rickard (2018) found "given the strong evidence for its memorial benefits, many cognitive and educational psychologists now classify testing as among the most effective educational techniques discovered to date." Although some teachers avoid exam-style questions in favor of quizzing in classroom environments, knowledge transfer is most likely to happen when the format of the knowledge has been created in alignment with the format of the end test. While testing remains effective it must be accompanied by feedback or more than the correct answers. Feedback is a key strategy when amplifying student learning in mathematics.

Students need to know why their answer is wrong and how to improve on it. Summative assessments need to have opportunities for student contributions to be reflected and adapted for them to be effective (Black & Wiliam, 2008; Pan & Rickard, 2018).

Assessment Practice and Feedback

Repeated testing can be adopted to provide evidence of student progress over time. There is accountability attached to teachers to provide evidence of student progress. Although, summative assessments can become formative if reflection, feedback, and action is taken based on the test taken. Summative tests may be employed at the end of the topic or semester. Teacher feedback and student reflection may inform the next teaching cycle with this test result and in turn, the summative test becomes formative in output. The linear nature of GCSE exams in schools means that students need to become familiar with this testing process. GCSE exams are written by teams of question writers and robustly tested before being given to students. The question language is carefully constructed. In-class questions by the teacher can often be more informal in language. Although ensuring material is accessible to students, time is needed to familiarize them with the language of the GCSE exam. The language used in GCSE exams is specific to the summative assessment and more formal than students may be used to. (Chambers, 2010; Marinho, Leite & Fernandes, 2017).

Table 3.1

Instructional Strategies Grounded in Research for Math Instruction

Instructional Strategy Theme	Research Proving Collaboration Amplifies Student Learning	Strategies
Modeling	• Dunlosky et al., 2013 • Chambers, 2010	Creating worked examples to share with students
Retrieval practice	• Roediger et al., 2011 • Karpicke & Blunt, 2011	Active learning opportunities for students to retrieve content
Exam practice including feedback and language	• Black & Wiliam, 2008	Turning summative tests into formative approaches

Strategy Integration with EdTech Tools and Instructional Application Vignettes

The teaching environment as we know it is ever-changing. Education technology affords teachers new opportunities to amplify student learning in mathematics. Students will gain not only skills in the educational technology deployed in their classroom but digital skills that can be adopted in their future careers. Modeling by the teacher as a key strategy to amplify student learning in mathematics can be embedded in face-to-face lessons and online lessons, both synchronous and asynchronously. The expert teacher can be on hand to guide students when needed, and show them a way to answer the problem. Retrieving content previously taught can be accessed easily within face-to-face or online lessons with some preparation ahead of time by the teacher. Preparing and conducting summative tests online can prove challenging. Likewise reducing test anxiety for students when undertaking preparation too. These key strategies can be adopted with the use of EdTech tools to amplify student learning.

Strategy One - Modeling Integrated with EquatIO, Videos, and GIFs

Teachers can now gain access to additional tools to make providing worked examples easier. EquatIO by Texthelp is one example that provides teachers with a full equation editor that is also intuitive. Teachers can not only write material with ease, they can ask students to submit work using EquatIO. EquatIO has touch screen handwriting recognition. Teachers and students can digitally write mathematics via their keyboard or handwritten notes. By accessing the EquatIO mobile feature handwritten mathematics on paper can be scanned in and converted to editable typed mathematics problems. EquatIO also supports speech to type mathematics meaning there are multiple methods for teachers to model correct answers for students, as well as being accessible to those with additional needs. The Mathspace feature of EquatIO allows students to collaborate and amplify their learning. This integrates into various Learning Management Systems (LMS), including Google Classroom.

When teaching mathematics online, teachers want to be the expert teacher for their students when they are outside the classroom. How can teachers demonstrate that paper-based expert modeled answer in an online format? It can be noted that the increased use of video by teachers may suggest video has been adopted as a go-to tool for modeling (Sutaro et al., 2020). Yet, not all students can access videos, and many run out of mobile data. Learning online or outside the classroom requires students to have devices and internet access. In 2018 over 10% of the US population had no home broadband access. In 2021 in the UK, "11% of teachers overall report that more than 1 in 5 of their pupils do not have adequate internet access for learning" (Sutton Trust, 2021). This lack of access can make watching videos prohibitive to learners accessing the internet via mobile data. Streaming HD video can use three times as much mobile data compared to a streaming standard quality video. Therefore, it is critical to ensure students have access to high-speed internet when thinking about integrating streaming video for instruction.

However, there may be alternative opportunities for students who may not have consistently high bandwidth connections to the internet.

Graphic Interchange Formats (GIFs) are moving images that autoplay and loop. They appear similar to video but have no audio. GIFs use relatively small amounts of data in comparison to video and can be created to show modeled worked examples. As illustrated in Figures 3.1 and 3.2, a slide deck of the question can be inserted, and the initial beginning of the answer added as a piece of text. This can then be duplicated, and the answer expanded until fully correct.

Figure 3.1

QR code to an example percentages GIF

qrco.de/ampglobaledu61

Figure 3.2

Example Questions for Slides

Slide #	Question	Answer
1	Solve for y. $3y + 8 = 29$	Subtract 8
2	Solve for y. $3y + 8 = 29$	Subtract 8 $3y = 21$
3	Solve for y. $3y + 8 = 29$	Subtract 8 $3y = 21$ Divide by 3
4	Solve for y. $3y + 8 = 29$	Subtract 8 $3y = 21$ Divide by 3 $y=7$

In Microsoft PowerPoint, with one click teachers can export the slide deck that models the answer as a GIF. This GIF can then be inserted into a task or worksheet for students to refer to as their modeled example. In Google Slides, teachers can use a GIF maker add-on or visit talltweets.com and turn their modeled slide decks into gifs. These GIFs can then be inserted into tasks for students as an animated worked example that leaps off the page when they are set to work.

GIFs are recognized as image files in many formats, meaning they can be housed where videos cannot. An example is in a Google Jamboard where the gif can be uploaded as a background on frame one followed by student work on frame two. Students can then choose to refer back to the animated gif on frame 1 if they need to access the worked example. Google Forms also accepts gifs as an image file. Nested within the question, the GIF animates the model answer with the student question above and the answer box below. By making the GIFs via an original slide deck the inaccessibility of GIFs can be addressed. For students who use a text-to-speech screen reader, they can access the material via the original slide deck shared by the teacher.

"GIFs lend themselves well to the topic of Algebra. Teachers can model each stage of solving problems line by line via the slide deck and then convert it to a GIF."

GIFs lend themselves well to the topic of Algebra. Teachers can model each stage of solving problems line by line via the slide deck and then convert it to a GIF. Students can engage with the repetitive nature of the GIF. This modeled answer approach seeks to highlight to students how marks are awarded in the summative GCSE exam and promotes high standards for written mathematics work. Students can narrate the GIF as it plays exploring the reasons behind each step the teacher has taken in the modeled answer. Teachers can personalize their approach to their student groups highlighting previous class errors and misconceptions. When teachers personalize resources students perceive that the effort and care the teacher placed in the resource creation as the effort and care that the teacher is showing them (Palmer et.al, 2017).

A note from Becky: GIFs can be powerful in younger grades, especially as a follow-up to Math Talks. Teachers can create slides in the following order:

***Slide 1:** Presents a Problem*

***Slide 2:** Students share the steps taken to reach their answer (class consensus)*

***Slide 3:** Class answer (with steps)*

***Slide 4:** Class justification*

The teacher can then take these slides and turn them into a GIF for students to refer back to throughout the unit (and beyond).

Strategy Two - Retrieval Practice with Digital Flashcards Gamified

Spaced practice is participating in retrieval knowledge over periods of time with timed gaps in between retrieval points. Spaced practice needs to be carefully constructed and well planned. Students should engage with an activity, or math concept, to recall the previously taught information rather than re-reading the concept. Spaced retrieval practice encourages concepts to become more concrete in the student's long-term memory and can be recalled upon when needed

(Dunlosky et al., 2013). When learning new concepts in mathematics, students often need to connect previously taught concepts and apply them to the new topic. For example, when looking

at simplifying fractions students are required to have the knowledge of divisibility checks and the highest common factors in order to be successful at simplifying fractions. Teachers need to carefully create opportunities for students to recall the principles of identifying the highest common factors and divisibility checks. The link can then be made between this previously taught content and this new topic of simplifying fractions.

"When learning new concepts in mathematics, students often need to connect previously taught concepts and apply them to the new topic."

Gamification of lessons involves students being rewarded for engaging in activities. Teachers can embed elements of gamification into their lessons or create whole new game-based activities. Game-based activities are when students learn new content throughout a game.

Gamification is when elements of design are added to lessons to improve student engagement. Student motivation is increased when gamification elements are introduced into the classroom. Gamification elements help connect theory to practical activities for students, deepening their understanding. When students can make additional attempts to improve their score, not only is their self-efficacy increased but their engagement is also maintained for longer (Alsawaier, 2017).

For spaced retrieval practice to be effective, memory tasks should be reduced, and active tasks increased. This is where gamification can be a key part of instructional design. The challenge for teachers is to make the content feel new and engaging for students whilst spaced activities cover the same topics repeatedly. Quizlet is an online platform that utilizes a series of teacher-created flash cards. Once a series of flashcards are created, the Quizlet presents the same topics in many formats for students to engage with, making the activity feel new to students even though topics are repeated. Quizlet does this by representing each set of key terms in a new and engaging format via its eight modes. For example, students can engage with the topic of parts of a circle. The teacher creates the "study set" in Quizlet defining the key terms. In week one, students can complete a pair matching activity on the terms. For week two, students can compete in a live game as a low-stakes assessment of the same key terms. Last, for week three, students could undertake a low-stakes formative quiz of multiple-choice questions on the same terms all via the initial "study set" created by the teacher. Each mode in Quizlet affords teachers a low-stakes assessment opportunity of the same content.

Table 3.2

Quizlet Modes to Integrate into the Classroom

Learn	A mixture of multiple choice and writing questions increasing in difficulty.
Flashcard	Traditional memory tasks of recall cards.
Write	Students type the definition of the term shown on screen.
Spell	Students hear the terms and type what they hear.
Test	A mixture of multi-format questions, matching, missing words, multiple choice. (Can be printed as a pdf document too)
Match	A drag and drop game where students match terms and their definitions.
Gravity	Similar to Match but terms fall as asteroids.
Live	Random questions from the set of terms where students join via a code and all play live.

A further example is the topic of angle facts in geometry. In each of the terms in the set in Quizlet, an image can be inserted. In the memory tasks of recalling angle facts, teachers can create a "study set" in Quizlet with an image of each type of problem and write the fact as the definition. In the following examples in Figures 3.3 and 3.4, you can see an image and definition that can be added to a Quizlet "study set." Quizlet is also an intuitive platform, meaning that as you begin to type a term or definition, it will offer suggestions based on previous teacher entries.

Figure 3.3

An example image on a flashcard in a Quizlet study set

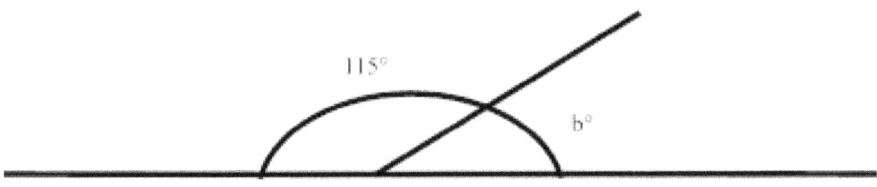

Figure 3.4

The definition added to the reverse of the flashcard in a Quizlet study set

Angles on a straight line add up to 180°

Once the "study set" is created teachers can then repeatedly assess via low stake quizzes, student knowledge of the key angle facts in geometry. Students can study this outside of the classroom asynchronously via a shared link. Autonomous students can engage and report back their scores on the games in Quizlet, for example, "gravity" and "match." Students can become competitive within the class of who can achieve the highest score. The link shared allows students multiple attempts to improve their score and their time engaged with the retrieval task is increased. By engaging with "gravity" and "match" students can enjoy gamified elements of their lesson and may experience increased motivation (Alsawaier, 2017). Within the live classroom, teachers can vary activities from playing "live" to all playing "match" and the fastest time wins.

Students learning through play and repeating the same material deepens their knowledge and strengthens their neural pathways for knowledge retention. When Quizlet was used with students learning vocabulary, they showed a significant improvement in test scores and reported the gamification of the lesson enhanced their learning experience (Sanosi, 2018).

Quizlet also houses a GCSE exam specification library for many subjects including mathematics. Written in conjunction with the major exam boards, teachers and students can specify their exam board and be given topic lists of activities that can be assessed via Quizlet. This exam integration helps with reducing teacher planning time. Teachers can be confident that the ready-made grab-and-go resources are endorsed by the exam board and will be of appropriate quality for their students.

Strategy Three - Repeated Exam Practice and Graphic Organizers

Exam practice can be embedded into lessons, but how often do we teach revision strategies to students? Often students select mass rereading of material as their strategy, which has little impact, especially if crammed before an assessment (Dunlosky et al., 2013). Teaching students how to revise can be as important as the content. The use of graphic organizers to detail their understanding of the topic can be a key tool for students. Graphic organizers support students linking prior knowledge to new material and develop their metacognition of the topic.

Graphic organizers can be paper-based or digitally held. Digitally held graphic organizers provide students with a ready-made revision bank of their notes that can easily be accessed when needed as illustrated in Figure 3.5. They can become living documents where students update regularly as they retain and recall different key information. Moving from paper-based graphic organizers to digitally held ones transforms student learning. Students can adapt and change their graphic organizers when new topics are introduced that connect to previously taught topics. (Casteleyn et al., 2013; Quigley et al., 2018).

Figure 3.5

Example fishbone graphic organizers utilized for math instruction

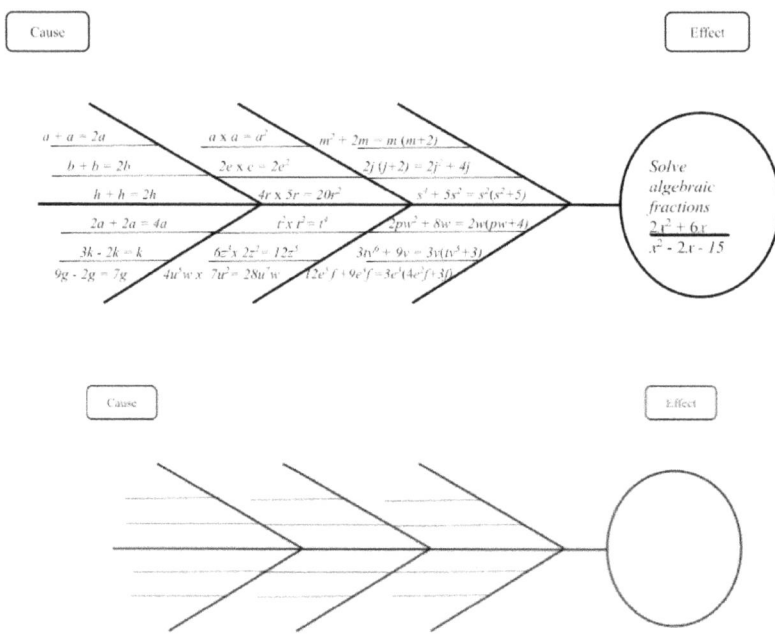

The use of this fishbone organizer allows students to build the bones of the fish with the aim of answering the final question in the circle. Students can see their end goal of answering the question and build their knowledge of the topics that are needed to answer this question. Using the fishbone graphic organizer aids students by building connections between topics through visually displaying related content. The use of graphic organizers forms part of exam practice for students developing their note-taking skills to facilitate preparation for exams. Students must become more familiar with the language of the GCSE exam and the format expected in their answers. In mathematics, students build on their mental knowledge and expand this into their written answers (Chambers, 2010). Students, therefore, need to become more familiar with the language features of the exam. This familiarity with the language of the questions may ease anxieties as students become more accustomed to what is required of them. The self-efficacy of students is often determined by the perceived difficulty of the task that has been set. Student motivation is increased when feedback is on effort and progress made rather than absolute metrics of the task taken (i.e., pass or fail) (EEF, 2018).

"The self-efficacy of students is often determined by the perceived difficulty of the task that has been set."

MathsKitchen.com is a website of GCSE exam-style questions that can be utilized to develop practice exercises and activities. Students can attempt them asynchronously or synchronously. Their responses are marked as correct or not, after being given additional opportunities to check their answer. This incorrect or correct feedback is accompanied by a supportive video with a modeled worked example by a mathematics teacher to help students understand why their answer is wrong. MathsKitchen.com also includes an assessment section. Here, students specify the time that they have for the task, for example, ten minutes.

MathsKitchen.com then creates an assessment for that time period but randomizes topics as they would appear in the summative GCSE exam.

A note from Matt: Khan Academy is a great alternative to MathsKitchen.com and is widely used in the US. Khan Academy provides video tutorials, digital lessons, and practice assessments for every subject and most grade levels.

Additionally, lessons can be posted on all major LMS's for students to complete or to go to as an additional resource to practice skills and concepts covered in class.

Students who combine graphic organizers and MathsKitchen.com can make notes on specifics of exam-style questions to build connections between their knowledge and the application to their exam. Gamification elements can be included by creating a leaderboard of time spent on MathsKitchen.com. In rewarding the effort made by the students this gamification element can increase student motivation to study independently (Alsawaeir, 2017). School-wide initiatives can be created by the adoption of whole school leaderboards of the number of ten-minute exam practice assessments undertaken by students. By combining gamification elements with the formality of summative assessment, students may increase the time spent with exam-style content. MathsKitchen.com can also be used for formative assessment in class as an exit ticket, affording students the opportunity to apply the theory of the lesson to the practical exam-style questions they will encounter later. This familiarity will put students in a stronger position for their summative GCSE assessments.

CONCLUSION - AUTHENTIC LEARNING IN MATHEMATICS

Exams have long been a key measure for student success and although assessment may change in the future, present exams remain. Exam technique is partly that, technique, and partly confidence for students. The skill of the teacher in gearing students up to feel empowered to tackle the exam while ensuring content is covered and students have revised is a large undertaking but one which teachers tackle bravely. Through the use of graphic organizers, students can become more self-reliant on their own abilities and grow in confidence celebrating their growth. Exams create anxiety in some by the mention of the term. Exam-style content with modeled answers will help students garner that internal strength to succeed.

The importance of the expertise of the teacher in the role of teaching students is significant. Yet, the challenge to transfer knowledge from the expert to students has become more difficult. Modeling facilitates the challenge of imparting knowledge to teachers. It provides opportunities for teachers to narrate their why, deepening understanding for students. Students are facing digital challenges of varying degrees, by moving from instructional videos to modeling GIFs teachers can solve many of these problems and amplify student learning by creating new opportunities for students. Students can create their own GIFs to summarize their key reading and research when exploring new topics. Students can explore the file size comparison of a video compared to a GIF, deepening their digital citizenship, and recognizing the importance of caring for their own digital footprint.

Low-stakes spaced retrieval assessments breed familiarity for students with exam-style content. This spaced retrieval will support students in developing stronger retrieval points meaning their knowledge can be applied in new contexts more easily. The skills that they learn in mathematics today may be the skills they can apply to their chosen career in the future. The possibilities are endless.

EDITORS' CONCLUSION

Ms. White provides a very straightforward framework to help teach students mathematics. Ultimately, this framework is premised on strategies and integrations that are designed to help students build confidence in their skills to knowledge of the concepts they have learned to do well. Through the chapter, we provide a number of additional EdTech tools and resources to help facilitate Ms. White's framework.

As you progress through the chapter, you will have seen how to strategically model math skills and concepts. In today's world, Ms. White notes that interactive videos and GIFs can be posted on an LMS for viewing at any time. Therefore, students can always practice and see examples of how to solve various types of problems. Historically, this would not have been possible. Now, students can see how to solve problems they are practicing whenever they would like. In addition, several EdTech tools and digital flashcards like Quizlet can be employed to help students with retrieval practice. Retrieval practice strategically placed within your instructional design can facilitate major improvements not only in mathematical skills, but all concepts and skills covered and taught within school.

For this chapter, we believe many of the strategies and EdTech integrations outlined in this chapter can work for any subject or skill that is taught in education since the framework is premised on modeling and retrieval practice. Therefore, as you are finalizing your reading of this chapter, think about how these strategies and EdTech integrations can be utilized when your teaching other concepts and skills outside of mathematics.

Key Takeaways & Instructional Implications and Applications

- When teaching mathematics, provide spaced practice to help students build and remember concepts and skills over long time periods. Practice reigns as the most important facet to improve mathematical skills. Therefore, teachers need to provide numerous options to strategically practice within their instruction.
- Modeling and retrieval practices are two fundamental strategies that can build math skills. In addition, modeling can be conducted through interactive videos and bite-sized GIFs.
- Utilizing interactive slides can help students practice and receive direct feedback on math problems.
- Gamification of math practice and formative assessment can help increase student engagement and motivation.

- Graphic organizers can be a great way to help students practice problems that require a number of steps to solve.
- Utilizing an EdTech tool like Quizlet can help students practice mathematical concepts and skills through digital flashcards. Be sure to model how students can use digital flashcards throughout the school year. Additionally, create instructional time within your lessons for students to practice utilizing this method of practice.

ADDITIONAL EDTECH STRATEGIES FOR STUDENT ENGAGEMENT FROM EDUCATORS AROUND THE WORLD

Ritika Tyagi - India

Using Nearpod to Teach Math

During the lockdown, I was looking for a tool which would be a one-stop solution for all my students. I came across Nearpod. It helped me to create my own activities like quizzes, matching pairs, and "Draw It" activities. It helped in deepening student understanding and engagement through gamification. Especially for my Math lessons, I asked students to write all the steps using the Draw-it feature and thus I could see their work.

Nearpod also provides thousands of ready to teach, customizable lessons to choose from. The Quiz feature gives me immediate feedback for student understanding! It's great to measure the learning outcome of each student in a simple way.

I also use Nearpod's VR lessons to take students on a virtual field trip and to explain chapters like - "Polygons" and "Quadratic Equations." Students love seeing the real-life application of each topic in Mathematics. Interactive features offer deeper learning during direct instruction. It also has self-paced assignments, which can empower students. Finally, you can utilize Nearpod as a collaboration tool during math instruction as the drawing features allow for alternative forms of assessment.

Google for Education
Certified Innovator

**Professor Filomena
Pizzulli - *Italy***

**App-Smashing Jamboard and EquatIO to Amplify Math
Instruction**

Jamboard is an excellent tool for creating interactive learning activities for students. However, if you want to create math activities, Jamboard does not have many built-in math features, other than a small collection of shapes. Thankfully, there is a powerful tool, that is also free for educators, that can be used to easily add all sorts of mathematical manipulatives, symbols, and expressions to Jamboard, which is called EquatIO.

EquatIO is a toolbar from the Google Extension store that makes it super easy to create mathematical expressions, as well as a wide variety of math manipulatives, and insert them into Google Docs, Slides, Forms, Jamboard, and more. Symbols generated in this extension can be copied to these various programs on Google Workspace, which helps teachers plan and deliver math instruction to their students using these tools.

Libo Valencia - USA

Visualizing Math Concepts in Action with GeoGebra

GeoGebra is a very intuitive and user-friendly platform for both teachers and students. As someone who is passionate about math and teaches it both at the high school and college levels, I really enjoy GeoGebra's potential to visualize abstract math concepts. It's an amazing tool that can bring mathematical ideas to life. Below is an example from my calculus students at the college where we used GeoGebra to visualize thederivative within an optimization problem (i.e., https://twitter.com/MrValencia24/status/1448068676394041351).

GeoGebra is also a fantastic tool to give students some choice in how to approach a math problem. One day, I asked my geometry students at the high school to walk around their home and take a picture of something that looked like a parallelogram. Students then uploaded the picture to GeoGebra and using a method of their choice, they got to prove or disprove whether it was a parallelogram or not. Giving students some choice (on the picture and the method) contributed to high levels of engagement during this activity. Below are some samples of students' work when they were participating in this activity in class (i.e., https://twitter.com/MrValencia24/status/1374434972585496577).

CONCLUSION - AMPLIFY LEARNING: A GLOBAL COLLABORATIVE

AMPLIFYING AUTHENTIC LEARNING IN READING, WRITING, AND MATHEMATICS

This book provides you with innovative and creative instructional strategies in reading, writing, and mathematics while also keeping in mind that the strategies were interchangeable between content areas. Each strategy shared is based on research and has been utilized in the classroom. Instead of focusing on only theory, this book provides you with strategies that are successfully being practiced in classrooms around the world. EdTech also plays a large role in each chapter because technology is such a prevalent part of our and our students' daily lives and can now be used as a medium to deliver our instruction in new and innovative ways to amplify learning like never before. We hope that you are able to bring some of these strategies back into your classroom and begin amplifying your students' learning journey with meaningful technology.

Throughout the conclusion, we will focus on key themes of the book and book series in addition to providing avenues for continuing our learning and expanding our professional learning networks. First, we will discuss how the purpose of this book was focused on integrating research-based instructional strategies with EdTech to amplify instruction and student learning in reading, writing, and mathematics. Second, we will reiterate how the primary purpose of this book series is to compile strategies and of compiled strategies and EdTech integrations from a diverse group of educators across the world to amplify learning. Third, one of our goals will be to discuss some recommendations for taking these strategies and integrations and implementing them in your classroom, school, and district. Fourth, we will be providing avenues for continued learning and growing your professional learning network. We focus on our #AmpGlobalEdu hashtag and opportunities for expanding your professional learning network by connecting with fellow readers, contributing authors, and editors of this book. To finalize this book, both co-editors will provide their final thoughts on the learning journey we have all been on as we have navigated the innovative strategies and EdTech integrations from classrooms around the globe. We will be rounding out the conclusion by thanking all of our contributing authors for the amazing work they have provided for this project!

Purpose of this Book and Book Series

The primary goal of this specific book was to provide a vast array of instructional strategies and EdTech integrations to amplify how we teach reading, writing, and mathematics in modern classrooms. An assortment of strategies and integrations covers a set of interchangeable instructional strategies and EdTech integrations that can be utilized across all content areas and grade levels. Additionally, we believe much of what is discussed in this book can be replicated within online, blended, and traditional in-person classrooms across the world. Altogether, the strategies and integrations in this book provide a roadmap and toolkit for teaching these vital skills that are the foundation for navigating our world and being a lifelong learner.

Our goal with this book series is to learn from a vast array of talented and diverse educators around the world and integrate research-based instructional strategies with EdTech to navigate modern classroom settings. Education is currently at a crux of immense change, which requires diverse perspectives to create innovative solutions to solve the everyday challenges we face in classrooms. Ultimately, we hope many of our author's research and strategy integrations with EdTech tools help educators around the world tackle these challenges.

In addition to using this book to help us learn how to further integrate research-based strategies and EdTech, we wanted to learn from educators around the world. Having a diverse set of contributing authors provides different perspectives from what we would see in our own backyard school and district, state, or national educational system. Seeing different perspectives helps us mold our own practices in our school and classroom, but also helps us develop policies to solve problems in our own communities.

We are in this together as educators of our local and global communities. Our classrooms and schools may be located across the globe, but our mission is to help amplify our students' learning. We want to cultivate our classrooms and instruction to be places where learning is amplified. By learning from each other, we will further innovate our practices to put our students, colleagues, and professional learning networks in the best positions to succeed in this ever-changing world.

Ensuring Authentic Learning in the Classroom

At the beginning of this book, we discussed the need to bring authentic learning into the classroom. The strategies shared throughout this book provide clear pathways towards students taking ownership of their learning and connecting the learning with their personal lives. Social media is now more prevalent than ever in many students' lives and there are plenty of opportunities for teachers to bring a similar "social media" type setting into regular assignments. The rigor and lesson objectives should maintain a high-level expectation for students. Authentic learning is not about reducing and minimizing what students are taught but instead is focused on providing students with an understanding of content in a meaningful and relevant way.

Authentic learning requires creativity, innovation, and critical thinking. All of these are showcased throughout the three chapters in this book. As you begin integrating the different strategies into your classroom, consider how the strategies can be altered to meet your students in a meaningful way. We want you to come back to this book many times to find and engage students in new strategies centered around authentic learning in reading, writing, math, and all content areas. Thus, this book and book series goal is to be a continued resource for you to utilize and find new instructional and EdTech integrations for your classroom and school to improve your practice over time versus only in the present.

Building Your Professional Learning Network

We hope that your journey across the United States, United Kingdom, and the globe, through reading this book and book series, has allowed you to go beyond new ideas and strategies for your classroom. We also want this book to support you in building your Professional Learning Network (#PLN). In each contributing author bio we have included the author's Twitter and/or Instagram Handles, please connect with them by sharing ideas, asking questions, and following their upcoming projects. Through social connections, we can ensure that we are taking our professional learning beyond the four walls of our classroom or office. #PLNs allow us to collaborate with creative, innovative educators across time zones, grade levels, and content areas.

EdTech tools will continuously shift and alter over time to better meet the demands of our students. Trying to keep up with these shifts can be taxing and a bit unrealistic, if going at it solo. Join and engage with our global #PLN to take some of the burdens off of you and your team.

You've made it this far in reading, so let's make sure the learning journey does not stop here. Whether you are new to social media or have become #EduFamous on Twitter, we are all on this journey to support and amp up learning for students. Let's connect!

Expanding our Community

As you grow your #PLN and connect with the authors in this book, be sure to utilize and share out #AmpGlobalEDU. By including this hashtag, #AmpGlobalEdu, we can easily connect and support one another. We invite you to join past and upcoming podcast episodes, roundtables, panel sessions, Twitter chats, and any of our additional platforms as we dive into a deeper understanding of the EdTech tools and strategies shared in this book along with the new and updated tools and strategies. All sessions, episodes, and chats can be easily accessed by searching for #AmpGlobalEdu on Twitter or Instagram or by adding a column in Tweetdeck for

#AmpGlobalEdu. We invite you to join us in our expanding global community!

Final Notes from the Editors

As co-editors and curators of this book and book series, we have enjoyed every minute of working with our contributing authors and compiling this book and book series for educators throughout the world. Take a moment to read our final remarks for this book on *Amplifying Authentic Learning in Reading, Writing, and Mathematics* as we tried to bring an innovative group of educators together from across the world to provide our thoughts and analysis of their work in each chapter. As you have been an active learner throughout this book, so have we in the creation of this book. We can guarantee you that many of the strategies and EdTech integrations have also been added to our teaching toolkits as a result of reading this book as well as the other three books of this book series!

Matthew Rhoads, Ed.D. Our ability to read, write, and problem solve in mathematics are essential foundational skills all students need to navigate our ever-changing world Throughout the past three chapters, we have seen instructional strategies ranging from retrieval practice, spaced vs. mass practice, station rotation, reciprocal teaching, interactive video, and strategic direction instruction all coupled with EdTech tools that can deliver the instruction within in-person, blended, and online classroom settings.

Beyond just the strategies and EdTech tools, we were taken on a journey for students to authentically learn and demonstrate their learning by harnessing mediums such as social media, student portfolios, and online communities centered around causes to display and share student-created content.

The goal of this book was to not only show research-based strategies integrated with EdTech but to also share how we can build our student's agency and buy-in to what we are teaching them. Through this, we can help them see how their work can impact their local classroom community, their town and city, and even the greater world community we all live in. In Chapter Two, Dr. Ilko describes this thought process excellently in terms of how we are planning our instruction by asking questions related to who our students are, their interests, how can we grow together as a community, and how we can use technology to not only increase engagement but to also increase their agency while we are working to accomplish our instructional goals.

One major theme I took from this book is that byte-sized learning is the future. I believe Ms. White exemplifies this in Chapter Three by outlining a number of strategies that can be utilized in a byte-sized manner within our classrooms to increase our student's ability to retain mathematical concepts and skills they are taught. Her use of modeling mathematical problems using GIFs is a masterful integration that helps our students see how a problem is solved in a byte-sized manner in the age of byte-sized content in the age of Tik-Tok and social media stories. Moving forward with how we deliver our instructional strategies and EdTech integrations, we must focus on byte-sized learning as this will be a medium our students, regardless of age, are comfortable with and used to receiving content delivered to them.

To finalize my thoughts, the strategies and EdTech integrations discussed in each of these chapters are interchangeable in nature. This means the vast majority of them discussed in this book can be used teaching any skill or area of content. For example, retrieval practice can be used in mathematics to help students review the steps to solving a problem as well as how in English to learn and practice vocabulary words. Another example of this taking is with the strategy of reciprocal teaching. Reciprocal teaching can be utilized to help build students reading comprehension as they read a text as well as in a science lab. For reading, students are predicting, clarifying/questioning, and summarizing the text while during a science lab students create hypotheses, clarify their thinking during an experiment and further question phenomena they observe, and summarize their experience at the end of the lab and discuss their conclusions. As we can see, the strategies discussed are interchangeable, which makes the strategies and EdTech integrations in this book a powerful toolkit you can utilize to teach a wide variety of skills and content you are teaching your students!

Becky Lim, M.Ed. As an elementary educator, reading, writing, and math are at the core of my teaching background. I was excited to meet the contributing authors of these three chapters and was surprised with how much I have learned from each of them. All three authors bring a unique twist into their content focus and have a genuine passion for teaching and learning. While not all of the authors are focused on elementary school, the strategies shared were definitely able to be differentiated to meet students at each academic level.

Reading is a beast for most educators because it is multifaceted and students come into each grade level with varying levels of comprehension, fluency, decoding, etc. In chapter one, Dr. Toney set a clear focus on reading comprehension. She has a strong background in each area of reading, but wanted to provide focused strategies and a clear direction. She shared the work of Jennifer Serravallo, a leading reading strategist in education, and how she modifies the strategies to meet students' diverse reading and learning needs. Dr. Toney sets the tone for the book in this first chapter as her strategies are ready to be implemented into any reading classroom in K-12.

When it comes to implementing writing, there are a variety of tools, books, trainings, etc. on the "best" way to do so. In many cases, writing becomes a rote activity with minimal student voice. Dr. Ilko changes all of this in chapter two. The strategies shared focused solely on authentic learning and incorporating writing with the students in mind. Dr. Ilko's passion for teaching writing and meeting students' individual needs is contagious. I am genuinely excited to bring her research based, authentic learning writing strategies into more classrooms around the world.

Finally, in chapter three, Sammy White shares a variety of strategies that focus on the students first when teaching math. Through her years of teaching experience and EdTech training, her chapter showcased the benefits of bringing in GIFs over videos and providing assessment feedback and practice. One thing that really stood out to me in this chapter was that Sammy didn't just share the strategies used and why she used them, she provided the "how." There were clear steps for how to implement each strategy and reasoning behind the order of each step. The ideas shared were genuine and beneficial to students in all grade levels.

This book is broken apart by content area, but the underlying theme is authentic learning.

I am overjoyed with how well this second book in the series has come together and how many takeaways I had while reading each author's individual chapter.

FINAL THOUGHTS AND THANK YOU TO THE CONTRIBUTING AUTHORS

We hope this book and each of the included strategies and EdTech tool integrations from educators around the globe in the series of *Amplify Learning: A Global Collaborative* have been useful to you. Transforming education by integrating research-based strategies with EdTech tools will be an ongoing effort for us as we learn more research-based strategies and new EdTech tools as we progress into the future. We are excited to have amplified educators' practices and skills from around the world. Each contributing author was selected based on the outstanding work that they are doing in education and every single one of them far exceeded our expectations. Let's turn up the volume and continue sharing, connecting, and collaborating with educators on a global level! We want to continue amping up the voices of educators.

#AMPGLOBALEDU

To our contributing authors in this book on *Amplifying Authentic Learning in Reading, Writing, and Mathematics* and the *Amplify Learning: A Global Collaborative* book series, thank you for sharing your expertise and experiences with us and the world. Specifically for this book, thank you to Jennifer Toney, Janet Ilko, and Sammy White for your spectacular and groundbreaking work. Each of you made this book possible. Your research-based EdTech strategies and tools will be used by educators around the globe to better meet students' diverse learning needs and amplify their learning. Your voices and skills deserve to be amplified and we hope this book and *Amplify Learning: A Global Collaborative* book series opens the door for continuous global connections and opportunities.

Thank you,

Matthew Rhoads, Ed.D., and Becky Lim, M.Ed.

REFERENCES

Alsawaier, R. (2017). The Effect of Gamification on Motivation and Engagement. *International Journal of Information and Learning Technology. 35*(1), 55-79. doi: 10.1108/IJILT-02-2017-0009.

Aguado, B., & Newirth, R. (2003). *Paint me like I am teen poems by writers corps.* Harper Collins.

Black, P., & Wiliam, D. (2009). Developing the theory of formative assessment. *Educational Assessment Evaluation and Accountability. 5*(1), 7-74. doi: 10.1007/s11092-008-9068-5.

Bereiter, C., & Scardamalia, M. (1987). *The psychology of written composition.* Lawrence Erlbaum Associates.

Brooke, E. (2015). *Four keys to success using blended learning implementation models.* Lexia Learning. Retrieved April 3, 2021, from https://www.lexialearning.com/re-sources/white-papers/blended-learning-four-keys

REFERENCES

Casteleyn, J., Mottart, A., Valcke, M. (2013). The impact of graphic organisers on learning from presentations. *Technology, Pedagogy and Education. 22*(3), 283-301. doi: 10.1080/1475939X.2013.784621.

Chambers, P. (2010). *Teaching Mathematics.* London: Sage

Cervetti, G. (2019). Five decades of comprehension research: Informing the future. *Journal of Literacy Research, 51*(1), 123–131.

Dahlstrom, H. (2019, March). Digital writing tools from the student perspective. *Education and Information Technologies, 24*(2), 1563-1581. Retrieved April 18, 2021, from https://link. springer.com/article/10.1007%2Fs10639-018- 9844-x

Daniels, H. (2002). *Literature Circles: Voice and choice in book clubs & reading groups* (2nd ed.). Portsmouth, NH: Stenhouse.

REFERENCES

DeVoss, D., National Writing Project, Eidman-Aadahl, E., & Hicks, T. (2010). *Because digital writing matters: Improving student writing in our schools.* Jossey-Bass.

Dhawan, S. (2020). Online Learning: A Panacea in the Time of COVID-19 Crisis. *Journal of Educational Technology Systems, 49*(1), 5-22. https://doi.org/10.1177/0047239520934018

Dunlosky, J., Rawson, K. A., Marsh, E. J., Nathan, M. J., & Willingham, D. T. (2013). *Improving Students' Learning With Effective Learning Techniques: Promising Directions From Cognitive and Educational Psychology.* Psychological Science in the Public Interest, *14*(1), 4–58. https://doi.org/10.1177/1529100612453266

Engzell, P., Frey, A., & Verhagen, M.D. (2021). Learning loss due to school closures during the COVID-19 pandemic. *Proceedings of the National Academy of Sciences of the United States of America, 118*(17) 1-7. https://doi.org/10.1073/pnas.2022376118

REFERENCES

Evmenova, A. S., Regan, K., & Hutchinson, A. (2020, March 1). AT for Writing: Technology-Based Graphic Organizers With Embedded Supports. *Teaching Exceptional Children, 52*(4), 266-269. doi:10.1177/0040059920907571

Fisher, D., Frey, N., & Hattie, J. (2016). *Visible learning for literacy*. Thousand Oaks, CA: Corwin.

Fitzgerald, B. (2016). *"Encryption, Privacy and Security:*. FunnyMonkey. Retrieved 1 May, 2021, from https://funnymonkey.com/2016/encryption-privacy-and-security

Gale In Context. (2021, April 23). *Gale in context: Elementary*. Gale A Cengage Company. https://www.gale.com/c/in-context-elementary

Harvey, S., & Daniels, H. (2015). *Comprehension and collaboration: Inquiry circles for curiosity, engagement, and understanding* (2nd ed.). Portsmouth: Heinnaman.

Hattie, J. (2008). *Visible Learning*. Abingdon, Oxon: Routledge.

REFERENCES

Hattie, J. (2012). *Visible learning for teachers*. New York, NY: Routledge.

Hattie, J. (2015). The applicability of visible learning to higher education. *Scholarship of Teacher and Learning in Psychology, 1*(1) 79-91.

Henry, E., Hinshaw, R., Al-Bataineh, A., & Bataineh, M. (2020, July 19). Exploring Teacher and Student Perceptions on the Use of Digital Conferencing Tools When Providing Feedback in Writing Workshop. *Turkish Online Journal of Educational Technology, 19*(3), 41-50.

Hicks, T. (2013). *Crafting Digital Writing: Composing Texts Across Media and Genre.* Heinemann.

Karpicke, J., Blunt, J. (2011). *Retrieval Practice Produces More Learning than Elaborative Studying with Concept Mapping.* Science, *334*(6055), 453-453. doi: 10.1126/science.1199327.

Karpicke, J. D., & Bauernschmidt, A. (2011).
Spaced retrieval: Absolute spacing enhances
learning regardless of relative spacing. *Journal
of Experimental Psychology: American
Psychological Association Learning, Memory,
and Cognition, 37*(5) 1250-1257.

Kieschnick, W. (2017). *Bold School.* Rexford, NY:
International Center for Leadership in
Education.

Kinsella, K. (n.d.). *Structured and Accountable
Classroom Language Use Across the Curricula*
[Keynote].

Kinsella, K., & Feldman, K. (2005). Narrowing the
language gap: The case for explicit vocabulary
instruction. *Scholastic.* http://teacher.
scholastic.com/products/authors/pdfs/
Narrowing_the_Gap.pdf

Kittle, P. (2008). *Write beside them: Risk, voice, and
clarity in high school writing.* Heinemann.

REFERENCES

Laghari, A., He, H., Khan, A., Karim, S. (2018). Impact of video file format on quality of experience (QoE) of multimedia content. *3D Research. 9*(3), 1-11. doi: 10.1007/s13319-018-0191-x.

Lehman, C., & Roberts, K. (2014). *Falling in love with close reading.* Portsmouth, NH: Heinemann.

Louie, A.-L. (1996). *Yeh-Shen: A Cinderella story from China.* New York: Puffin Books. Maine, A. (2021). *Loom video web stories on YV* [how-to video on publishing web stories] [video]. Retrieved from: https://www.loom.com/share/a3c9bbb8e7254e8dbac06b683bf1eb23

Marinho, P., Leite, C., & Fernandes, P. (2017). Mathematics summative assessment practices in schools at opposite ends of performance rankings in Portugal. *Research in Mathematics Education, 19*(2), 184-198, doi: 10.1080/14794802.2017.1318085

McEwan, E.K. (2021, April 20). *Teach the seven strategies of highly effective readers*. All about adolescent literacy: Resources for parents and educators of kids in grades 4-12. http://www. adlit.org/article/19844/

McREL.org (2021, April 23). *RtI, PBIS, and MTSS: An evolution, a revolution, or roses by other names?*. McREL International. https://www.mcrel.org/rti-pbis-and-mtss-an-evolution-a-revolution-or-roses-by-other-names/?gclid=CjwKCAjwg4-EBhBwEiwAzYAlskJvZOJTfg61m6iTulZuf-NexiLlCPILb6ZW RnVhHsEwCrQTOxIOBm-RoCiF8QAvD_BwE

Morgan, H. (2015). Focus on technology: Creating and using podcasts promotes student engagement and learning. *Childhood Education. 91*(1) 71-73.

National Center for Education Statistics. (2020). *Fast facts*. https://nces.ed.gov/fastfacts/ display.asp?id=147

REFERENCES

National Council of Teachers of English (NCTE). (2019). *Definition of literacy in a digital age* [Position statement]. https://ncte.org/statement/nctes-definition-literacy-digital-age/

National Governors Association Center for Best Practices, Council of Chief State School Officers. (2010). *English language arts standards*. Common Core State Standards Initiative. www.corestandrs.org/ELA-Literacy

National Writing Project. (n.d.). *Youth voices.* Retrieved from www.youthvoices.live Palincsar, A. S. (2013). Reciprocal teaching. In J. Hattie & E. Anderman (Eds.), *International guide to student achievement* (pp. 369-371). New York, NY: Routledge.

Palmer, E., Lomer, S., & Bashliyska, I. (2017). *Overcoming barriers to student engagement with Active Blended Learning: Interim report.* University of Northampton.

REFERENCES

Pan, S., Rickard, T. (2018). Transfer of test-enhanced learning: Meta-analytic review and synthesis. *Psychological Bulletin. 144*(7), 710-756. doi: 10.1037/bul0000151.

Pearson, P. D., & Cervetti, G. N. (2015) Fifty Years of reading comprehension theory and practice. In P. D. Pearson, E. H. Heibert (Eds.), *Research-based practices for teaching common core literacy* (pp. 1-24). New York, NY: Teachers College Press.

Purcell, K., Buchanan, J., & Friedrich, L. (2013). *The impact of digital tools on student writing and how writing is taught in schools.* Pew Research Center.

Quigley, A., Muijs, D., and Stringer, E. (2018) *Metacognition and self-regulated learning: guidance report.* Education Endowment Foundation

Readworks. (2021, April 10). *Readworks.* Readworks. https://www.readworks.org/

REFERENCES

Roediger, H., Agarwal, P., Mcdaniel, M.,
McDermott, K. (2011). *Test-Enhanced Learning
in the Classroom: Long-Term Improvements
From Quizzing.* Journal of experimental
psychology. Applied. *17*(4). 382-95.
10.1037/a0026252.

Rosenblatt, L. (1978). *The reader, the text, the poem:
The transactional theory of the literary work.*
Carbondale, IL: Southern Illinois University
Press.

Rosenshine, B., & Meister, C. E. (1993). Reciprocal
teaching A review of 19 experimental studies.
Technical Report No. 574. Retrieved April 21,
2021 from https://www.researchgate.net/
publication/271429623_Reciprocal_Teach
ing_A_Review_o f_19_Experimental_Stud-
ies_Technical_Report_No_574

Sanosi, A. (2018). *The effect of quizlet on vocabulary
acquisition. Asian Journal of Education and e-
Learning. 6*(4). doi: 10.24203/ajeel.v6i4.5446.

Serravallo, J. (2015). *The reading strategies book.*
Portsmouth, NH: Heinemann.

REFERENCES

Sutarto, S., Sari, D., Fathurrochman, I. (2020). Teacher strategies in online learning to increase students' interest in learning during COVID-19 pandemic. *Jurnal Konseling dan Pendidikan.* *8*(3), 129-137. doi: 129. 10.29210/147800.

Sutton, T. (2021) *Remote learning: The digital divide - Sutton Trust.* [online] Sutton Trust. Retrieved from: https://www.suttontrust. com/our-research/remote-learning-the-digital-divide

Texas Education Agency. (2002). *Comprehension instruction.* Reading initiative. https://tea. texas.gov/sites/default/files/redbk2.pdf

Texas Education Agency. (2021). *Key comprehension strategies to teach.* Reading rockets. https://www.readingrockets.org/ article/key-comprehension-strategies-teach

United Nations. (2020). *Policy brief: Education during COVID-19 and beyond.* Retrieved May 1, 2021, from https://www.un.org/development/desa/dspd/wp-content/uploads/sites/22/2020/08/sg_policy_brief_covid-19_and_education_august_2020.pdf

Wilkinson, I. A. G., & Son, E. H. (2011). A dialogic turn in research on learning and teaching to comprehend. In M. L. Kamil, P. D. Pearson, E. B. Moje, & P. Afflerbach (Eds.), *Handbook of reading research* (Vol. IV, pp. 359–387). New York, NY: Routledge.

LIST OF TABLES

LIST OF FIGURES

CONTRIBUTING AUTHOR BIOGRAPHIES

Jennifer Toney

Jennifer Toney is a United States-based educator who teaches in Western Pennsylvania. She is a third grade English Language Arts teacher at the Sharpsville Area School District where she focuses on digital and analog blended learning approaches to grammar and writing in a gamified writing workshop. Jennifer is also an adjunct instructor at the Westminster College Graduate School of Education. She received her doctorate in Curriculum and Instruction with a focus in literacy at Kent State University in 2017, where she conducted her research study, "Third Grade Students' Literacy Practices As They Compose Multimodal Texts In A Digital Writing Workshop". Her scholarly interests include multimodal composition in the elementary classroom, blended learning approaches to writing workshop with young writers, and English Language Arts curriculum development in the K-5 setting. Prior to teaching third grade English Language Arts, Jennifer taught for several years in kindergarten, first, and second grade primary classrooms. In addition to "Amplified Learning: A Global Collaborative", Jennifer has written as a contributing author to the Rowman & Littlefield series, "Comic Connections" and the Keystone State Literacy Association journal, Pennsylvania Reads. Learn more about Jennifer by visiting her website:
https://sites.google.com/view/jennifertoney/biography or contacting her on Twitter: @JENTONEY.

Janet Ilko

Janet Ilko Ed.D. is an educator with over three decades of experience spanning K-12 classrooms. She has been an academic coach, elementary teacher, middle school humanities and ELD teacher, and a program manager for an independent studies program for grades 9-12. Her doctoral work with Long Term English learners focused on the effect of relevancy and rigor on student academic success, sharing the findings through a variety of professional developments and articles. Her current work at the high school level is focused on literacy engagement with students grade 9-12, providing specialized language supports for students with an emphasis on struggling readers and second-language learners. She recognizes and fosters the importance of student and family engagement, access, and support in teaching and learning in online environments, ultimately seeking "techquity" for all students.
Twitter: wrtin4change

Website: www.writinginmyhand.org

Sammy White

Sammy studied secondary mathematics as her teaching specialism and has been enjoying teaching secondary mathematics now for over 10 years. Sammy has led the development of mathematics teaching across a large college group developing early career and experienced teacher's mathematics teaching skills. Sammy now works as an education consultant supporting schools and colleges in upskilling mathematics staff and embedding maths across their whole school curricula. Sammy is a Google for Education Innovator and the first female Google for Education Coach in Europe. Sammy is a GCSE mathematics examiner and an ambassador for Common Sense Education. Sammy blogs at www.whatthetrig.co.uk and can be found @WhatTheTrigMath on Twitter.